A Tale of Two Dusters
and Other Stories

Road Dog Publications was formed in 2010 as an imprint of Lost Classics Book Company and is dedicated to publishing the best in books on motorcycling for the thoughtful rider.

A Tale of Two Dusters and Other Stories
© August 2013, Kirk Swanick, All Rights Reserved.

ISBN 978-1-890623-40-1
Library of Congress Control Number: 2013948927

An Imprint of Lost Classics Book Company

This book also available in e-book format at online booksellers. ISBN 978-1-890623-41-8

A Tale of Two Dusters and Other Stories

By Kirk Swanick

Road Dog
PUBLICATIONS

Publisher
Lake Wales, Florida

In memory of C. S. "Red" Swanick,
father, teacher, mentor and above all, friend...
without whom none of this would have been possible.

ABOUT THE AUTHOR

Kirk Swanick was born and raised in northeastern Illinois, in the northern Chicago suburb of "Mudsville", also known as Mundelein, Illinois.

Kirk has been fascinated with the "infernal" combustion engine as long as he can remember, or possibly even before that. He began tinkering with things mechanical long before he should have. He cut his teeth on bicycles, which was soon followed by mini-bikes and motorcycle engines. Next came cars, then ultimately aviation (which turned into a career). Eventually he returned full circle back to motorcycles where his passion for repairing and restoring the Japanese import bikes of his youth is only eclipsed by his passion for riding them. He is also an avid black powder firearms enthusiast, shooter, and tinkerer/amateur gunsmith. He resides on a number of black powder internet forums as administrator, moderator, and advisor, as well as a number of motorcycle-based forums primarily concerned with the bikes he owns and restores. He is also a hunter, archer, reloader and unsung guitar-slinger.

He attended Mundelein High School and after graduation

attended College of Lake County for two years until deciding he wanted to make a career of fixing things that go fast and make noise, with aviation earning top billing in that department. He attended Spartan School of Aeronautics in Tulsa, Oklahoma, and graduated from their Aviation Maintenance Technician program earning an AMT degree and receiving his Federal Aviation Administration Airframe and Powerplant license in late 1979. He received his FAA Inspection Authorization in 1984 and has kept it in constant currency since. Presently he is part-owner of Waukegan Aviation Services/Waukegan Avionics, a licensed FAA Repair Station, avionics dealership, and full-service piston aircraft maintenance and service center.

Kirk resides with his wife, son, daughter-in-law, and granddaughter in Waukegan, Illinois, just shy of the Wisconsin border, where he loves to spend more hours riding his motorcycles than would be considered advisable by any licensed marriage counselor.

He has taken and completed both the Motorcycle Safety Foundation (MSF) Basic Rider Course (BRC) and Experienced Rider Courses (ERC).

Foreword

A Tale of Two Dusters and Other Stories

Road Dog Publications publishes books "...for the Thoughful Rider," so you may ask, "What's all this stuff about cars?!" that you will find in this book.

I first met Kirk Swanick through an Internet motorcycling forum we both freqent. The bike stories I read there by Kirk were more than just thread starters, they were complete stories that had more to do with the internal experience of riding motorcycles than the external, and which usually had me laughing out loud in front of my computer screen, while my wife, hearing me from her perch in the next room, wondered what in the world I was doing in the office. I read thread after thread, and Kirk's quality of writing was consistent and book-worthy. I mentioned to Kirk that he might want to put these stories together in book form. So many forum members had commented on the quality and humor of the writing that I felt sure the larger public would welcome a printed version with all the stories in one place.

Then I read his "Tale of Two Dusters" story on a forum for afficionados of all things "A Body" (Chrysler/Dodge/Plymouth's designation for the body style of the Valiant, Barracuda, Demon, Charger, and Duster, among others), where the author was known as "Captain Kirk," and found it every bit as enjoyable a read as his motorcycling posts and it even had a sprinkling of motorcycle episodes thrown in among all the tales of carbs, trannies, and hi-performance exhausts.

Tinkering around on hot rods has significant similarities to doing the same on motorcycles for those of us who struggle working on and modifying old bikes. If you've ever wrenched on your bike you will relate to this story of wrenching and modifying a car just as well. Once a motorhead, always a motorhead, regardless of machine.

And if you, like many riders, have had your years of youthful hooliganism on bikes, then you will relate as well to the hooliganism of hot rodding and all the craziness that goes along with it. They're related and only separated by two wheels.

So, into the mix went the Duster story, followed by other stories directly concerned with vehicles of the two-wheeled variety.

Enjoy the ride.

—Michael Fitterling, Publisher

TABLE OF CONTENTS

A TALE OF TWO DUSTERS

PROLOGUE

The story began back in 1975 when I bought my first Duster; a '72 340 "Mr. Norm's" car. For those of you unfamiliar; Mr. Norm's Grand Spaulding Dodge was *the* Midwest's premier muscle car dealer, if not the entire country's.

An acquaintance of mine got it from somewhere; I actually got to see it and ride in it shortly after he acquired it, having no idea I would someday own it, and it me. It was painted a bright "Tor-Red" and had the Duster Rallye Package with 340 decals and stripes with the little pissed-off looking tornados on it, Rallye wheels with Goodyear E-60s, 3.91 8¾ rear end with hi-lift shackles, air shocks, black split bench seat, three speed tranny on the floor with Hurst Indy shifter, 340 cubic-inch V-8 motor with the mammoth-sized Carter Thermo-Quad four barrel carb and headers.

I ended up with it because the guy I got it from was not much of a driver and too much of a partier. He had two separate accidents; the first time he ran off the road and rolled it up on its left side in a ditch, which (surprisingly enough) did very little damage other than push in the left rear quarter panel along with some collateral damage to the driver's door and left front fender. He and his buddies managed to roll it back onto all fours and drive it home, after which he continued to do what he did best; party and drive poorly.

Shortly thereafter, he managed to drive off the road and plant it into the corner of some poor soul's house in the middle of the night. It was pretty banged up in the front, but still ran, and the radiator, unbelievably, did not leak. It was at this point that I was able to pick it up fairly cheap. (He needed the money for his court appearance...go figure. Justice has a funny way of coming around the corner and sayin', "Howdy do.")

I went to pick up the car at the lot to which it had been towed after the "altercation." About halfway home the hood popped open—as in vertical (you know; like, straight up and down?!)—bending the hinges in the process. The latch had been bent in the accident, I guess, and wasn't up to the drive home...which I found out at highway speed. So, I forced it back down to where I could at least see over the now-buckled hood, and tied it down with a length of rope I found in the trunk (Yee-Hah! Feelin' like a true redneck now!) and managed to make it home without further incident. I pulled into the driveway of my parents' house, rolled it up the driveway to the empty garage, and switched off the motor. Seems strange that the first thing one would do after buying a car would be to tear it apart; but that was my plan.

So now it was time to get down to business. The buckled hood came off, then out with the engine and tranny. I had the motor down to gaskets and bolts in about three days. The biggest surprise was finding the huge domes of a set of TRW

13:1 pistons ogling me from the bores in the block once I'd pulled the first head. *"Uhhh...don't think those are stock, kiddies..."* Pop-Tops—a Mr. Norm's freebie! It was sort of like the feeling you would get upon opening an old wooden trunk you just found up in the attic, covered by a very dusty old tarp, and seeing the frazzled fuses of four sticks of dynamite silently staring up at you— *"Be vewwy, vewwy, careful..."* The headers were pretty much junk, dented and pinched from the accident, so reluctantly I pitched 'em in the garbage. That hurt, but I got over it. The motor parts went to Sexton Automotive in Crystal Lake, Illinois, for rework. Meanwhile, I started in on the bodywork.

A Tale of Two Dusters
Chapter 1

The Journey Begins

It was obvious the hood was beyond help, so it began a pile known as "junk." The deck lid (trunk) was rusted through along the bottom edge, so off with its head as well. The front fenders, while both damaged, looked repairable, so I pulled them both off and began the tedious job of pounding out the dents as best I could and body grinding and applying body filler. I was fairly new to the whole Bondo/filler thing and botched it up a couple of times; until my good friend Mike, a recent grad of Wyoming Tech body and fender tech school, showed me the magic trick of globbing on the filler heavy, then shaving it before it hardened completely with a Sureform file, instead of worrying about trying to shape it with the rubber spatula-thingy that comes conveniently tucked inside the plastic mixing cup they so nicely perch on top of the can. This really stepped up production. You could be a complete buffoon and still get it right. (Not that I'm admitting to being a buffoon, mind you. In fact, I can't even tell you what a buffoon is; maybe a cross between a bassoon and a baboon? Or maybe a buffer and a raccoon? I still don't know to this day.) Meanwhile, I was scavenging through all the local bone-yards and finally scrounged up a faded metallic-blue Demon deck lid, an orange Duster hood, and a rust-free quarter panel from a vinyl-topped Gold Duster. The whole quarter panel thing was an interesting piece of work; the guy at the bone-yard just cut the whole section off with a Sawz-All and gave me the whole chunk! Sort of like hacking off a chunk of cheese with your pocket knife and stuffing it in your cheek. I managed to scrounge up a couple of good, straight hood hinges while I was there, as well. I was managing to collect a nice pile of junk in the corner of the garage by this time.

The original rear quarter panels had some small rust holes back behind the rear wheels. I glassed and filled the ones on the right quarter. The left side didn't concern me because I would be replacing the entire left quarter panel with the scavenged Gold Duster quarter from the bone-yard.

It really didn't take all that long to get the deck lid, new hood and hinges, and front fenders back on. Now, the quarter panel; that was a horse of a different color. (No, *really*. It was *gold!*) I often wondered what sort of person would have owned or driven a Gold Duster, but then decided it wasn't worth wasting thought on. With Mike showing me what to do (or more importantly, what NOT to do), we drilled out the spot welds around the perimeter of the trunk, rear panel, and door jamb. We chewed up more than a few quarter-inch drill bits; those spot welds were tough as friggin' nails. Then we took an air chisel, found the lead-filled seam where the roof panel joins the quarter panel, and let 'er rip. After peeling away the quarter panel skin there was this split-second of horror (on my part) of "Oh, man…what the hell did we just do?" Probably a common thought when one is gaping at three-quarters of a car, I'm guessing. (Notice how I use the word *we* here. I'm not taking the rap on this one alone.) Well, too late now to turn back. So we did the same thing to the mangled corpse of a quarter panel from the Gold Duster donor part. Once we peeled off the remains of the hideous vinyl top and removed the glue, we trimmed the roof line panels to overlap. On the Gold Duster donor panel, I just heated up the roof joint with a propane torch and melted the lead filler right out of there, and the two panels just separated like a couple of tired, old Legos. After a dozen or so mock-ups, edge trimmings, trial fittings, etc., I finally felt the quarter fit, and it looked like I wanted it to, so we drilled a couple of "strategically-placed," one-eighth inch holes and secured the replacement skin in place with a few pop-rivets to jig it up. Then we began the tedious task of filling each one of the spot weld holes we'd drilled out with a molten pool of gleaming brass, using a borrowed oxy-acetylene torch and brazing rod. Of course, the holes in the donor skin didn't line up with the holes in the old structure; this is exactly the result we wanted. The actual install time for the quarter, once we passed the *"D'oh!"* barrier, was surprisingly short.

The hardest part for me was blending the roof line seam with the quarter. We chose to use body filler instead of lead; it was easier to manage (Hot molten lead runs down-hill; duh!), but I must have done that seam at least ten times before I was satisfied. I remember despairing over it; feeling like I'd never get it right. I'll clue you in right now; I'm a hopeless perfectionist who can't stand shoddy workmanship and I wasn't any different back then. After much hair-pulling and many do-overs, I finally got it to where I was satisfied. I learned one neat trick. The pop-rivets we'd used to secure the new quarter, of course, stuck out "proud" of the surface. We simply backed up each pop-rivet with a socket on a breaker bar and smacked the pop rivet with the business end (round side) of a ball peen hammer until we'd dented it down below surface level, then simply filled in the dent with body filler. POOF! Gone. Rivet? What rivet?

Next, I began the really nasty job of scraping and wire-wheeling the underside of the car. Once I got all the lousy, peeling factory undercoating and rust off, I yellow zinc-chromate-coated the entire underside and then re-coated it with Westley's spray can undercoating. All the rear suspension parts got de-greased, wire wheeled, then got a couple coats of gleaming white Rust-Oleum enamel, including the rear end, drive shaft, springs, shackles, and shocks. The gas tank came out and got undercoated as well, along with the tank hanger brackets. I was determined that rust was not going to be an issue in the future. (Not that it mattered; as you'll see later.)

The engine bay and K-frame were in pretty good shape; remember, this car was only three years old at the time. I de-greased, wire wheeled and rattle-canned the engine bay with Tor-Red touch-up paint and repainted the K-frame and front suspension parts with black Rust-Oleum as original. Things were really starting to shape up. It was starting to look like a car again. Minus a motor, of course.

———————

Meanwhile, back at the ranch...

Things were cookin' on the motor stove. The block had been degreased and acid-dipped, new cam bearings and freeze plugs installed, and it was honed to standard bore (4.04). The cast crank was polished, radiused, and the oil holes chamfered and de-burred. I reused the TRW 13:1 pistons with Speed Pro rings, which only came in .030 oversize at the time, and I had to meticulously hand-file each one for the proper ring end gap. Back in those days I had no fancy ring-filer thingy like these spoiled kids today can get with a Summit catalog and Daddy's credit card. Ahh, the memories! It filled many an evening when I could have been out doing those things that eighteen-year-olds do (and probably shouldn't). Looking back, it probably kept me out of trouble. Anyway, it was cold and wintery out there, so I got this bright idea to assemble the motor downstairs in Dad's basement workshop where it wasn't (wintery, that is). All the parts were meticulously masked, trimmed, and painted with Pontiac Blue engine enamel; the auto parts store was fresh out of Chrysler Blue, and, being eighteen and rather impatient, I decided not to wait for the next shipment and picked the closest thing to it. I liked the sky-blue Pontiac color better anyway. The heads had been CCed to lower the compression to a more "streetable" 11.5:1, ported and polished, knurled valve guides and springs shimmed to go with the cam my shop had selected for me. The cam was an Automotive Alliance (????-probably some generic brand at the time) grind with .450/.475 lift and 298/308 duration, topped off with a new set of Melling lifters. The engine was assembled with Federal Mogul bearings reusing the original rod bolts and nuts, and oil pan. I stuck in a Melling Hi-volume oil pump. The heads went on using Fel-Pro, Pro Blue gaskets.

———

Where was I?

Oh, yeah, the engine.

So I got the bottom end all together, then buttoned up the heads and valve train. Due to costs, I stuck with the stock push rods and rocker arms and shafts. I had purchased, used, an Offenhauser 360 manifold (out of the newspaper) from some Navy guy stationed at the Great Lakes NTC who was being transferred somewhere else, so I cleaned it up and got ready to bolt it on, when I discovered it was NOT for a 318 as the guy had promised, but for an early 273. The intake ports matched up fine, but the manifold bolt holes were drilled at a *different angle*. Of course the seller was long-gone by the time

I discovered this. Discouraged and running low on funds, I decided to simply port-match the stock cast-iron four-barrel manifold to match the head ports and gaskets (bad idea). I got through maybe three or four ports before I burned up my Dad's brand new Craftsman grinder. Like I said—bad idea.

This was really starting to suck. Fortunately, a friend of a friend knew a guy that had an Edelbrock Torker 340 X-type, aluminum, high-performance manifold with a pair of polished aluminum Edelbrock M/T (Mickey Thompson) valve covers to match, and he let them go sinfully cheap ($40 comes to mind). They fit like a glove and looked a hell of a lot better, too. This created another dilemma, though. I had originally planned on re-using the monster Thermo-Quad, four barrel carb with its sewer pipe-sized secondaries. But the Edelbrock manifold had no choke well provision for the choke coil assembly. Maybe Einstein could have figured out some way to rig up a manual choke to work with this setup, but I didn't have the patience. Turned out I didn't need it.

One of my friends just happened to have a Holley 600 single-pumper vacuum secondary carb that had been in an engine fire. Aside from being really sooty and in need of a rebuild, it looked like a good bargain, since he gave it to me free. It fit the square-bore Torker mounting flange without using an adapter plate, too, as it was a square-bore carb, where the TQ was a spread-bore.

After going through the Holley and bolting the flywheel onto the motor, I decided it had warmed up enough to get the motor off the stand and get the longblock out into the garage, bolt on the clutch pack and tranny, and drop it in. There was just one hitch:

Q: How do you get a 400+ pound longblock up a (long) flight of basement stairs, out the back door, down the stoop, and out into the garage?

A: With great difficulty!

I believe that could quite possibly be the understatement of the year. My buddy, Howard, and I almost ruined forever our chances of having offspring in later years.

My Mom's freshly painted basement stairs suffered silently as we heaved and strained, gonads shrieking and spinal discs writhing in mortal agony. Whose stupid, freakin' idea was this anyway?!!!! One step at a time, we finally got it out the back door, our voices at least an octave higher, when one of us lost our grip (I'll blame it on Howard, as he's not here to defend himself.) and dropped the damn thing on the back stoop. Amazingly, it didn't do much to the motor except scratch the fresh Pontiac-Blue paint a little and maybe put a tiny dent in the pan. The concrete stoop was not so fortunate, losing a two-inch chunk off one of the step corners. Ooops! Whose stupid, freakin' idea...oh. We covered that.

Undaunted, we lurched and grunted and heaved the longblock out into the garage. My back has never been the same. My family jewels apparently made a full recovery...as evidenced by my kids.

So, I managed to get the new Borg-Warner street/strip clutch and pressure plate bolted on, next came the bell housing and tranny. All dressed up in new paint; the bell housing wearing Tuxedo Black and the tranny standing out in stark contrast in brilliant Rust-Oleum White, all bolted to a fresh Pontiac Blue motor, topped off with polished, finned aluminum rocker covers and an X-Plane Torker aluminum manifold. *I* was impressed, anyway. Let the transplant begin.

Now let me tell you about the way an eighteen-year-old thinks. If it works, it's OK. This was pretty much our mantra back then. This theory applied to my engine hoisting technique as well. I had wrapped a big logging chain around one of the two-by-six joists in the garage and hung a two-ton cable come-along from the chain. Won't work, you say? The joist will collapse? Oh, I'm much smarter than that, Mister! I'll just wedge a four-by-four under the joist on either side of the car to support it! It worked, too, except...

The come-along hoisted the motor nicely into the air, and we pushed the car under it. Now, this particular come-along had a kind of toggle switch on its side: flipping the switch either one way or the other allowed you to raise or lower whatever it was that was "comin' along." It worked fine when I pulled the engine out. What I didn't know was...the switch-thing was sort of squirrely. (You know where this is going, right?) If you didn't get it ALL the way in the opposite direction, well...if you've ever gone fishing with your trusty Zebco 404 and released the button with a heavy sinker on the line...

Fortunately, the only damage was to one of the shifter fork threaded rods coming out the side of the tranny. Needless to say, the motor did not get bolted in that fine, sunny day. It took a week of waiting for a new shifter fork and another bottle of gear oil before I went down that road again. Can you believe I used the same come-along AGAIN to drop the motor in? (Maybe "drop" the motor is not such a good term.) Anyway, this time it went off without a hitch. It was in! A few short hours of hooking up the water pump, radiator, carb, headers and distributor and I was ready to pull the pin on the little blue grenade!

I had gone through all the usual bullshit of pre-oiling the engine, setting the initial timing, etc, etc. One expects to encounter some difficulties, natch', so I had the fire bottle standing by in the ready hands of Howard with a death-grip on it, and I was really nervous as I sucked in a deep breath and finally twisted the key. The motor lit immediately...no cranking, no farting or popping...it was just RUNNING and, Lordy, was that puppy LOUD!!!!!!!! Idling at about 2000, the sound waves were reverberating off the brick walls of the house. Howard and I were grinning like a couple of Cheshire cats; and, when I shut it down, my ears were ringing like church bells on Sunday morning! The heat from the open headers had melted off some of my fresh undercoating, but standing there, hearing the engine ping, pop, and tick as it cooled down, smelling raw gasoline and exhaust mingled with the baking of fresh engine paint, there was *no* better place in the whole world to be! We were in Motor Heaven!

A Tale of Two Dusters
Chapter 2

Teething Pains

So, now, once you've got a bad motor shoehorned into a car, whaddya do with it?

Break it in.

So I did. I hung a set of Turbo Thrush header mufflers on the business ends of the Kustom headers and headed out for the open road to put lots of break-in miles on the motor. The body was still pretty rough; blue trunk lid, primer-gray quarter panel, and primer on the fenders where I'd Bondo'd them. I left the hood off initially to show off the motor; it looked pretty good. No; it looked DAMN good!, which was in stark contrast to the rest of the car.

I quickly racked up a couple hundred 55mph plus break-in miles, to the point where the rings were probably seated and I felt comfortable rompin' on it a little.

So what do you do with a tight, broken-in motor?

Tune it, of course!

Tuning was fun. It was an excuse to tinker and fiddle with minute details such as timing advance or vacuum secondary opening, jetting, etc. and then go romp on it to check my work. I did a lot of tuning. I did a lot of romping on it, too.

Legal Disclaimer: All you punk kids take note. Don't go romp on your car. It's bad. Any mom, grandma, or cop will tell you so. Just because I did it and got away with it (enjoying the crap out of myself) is no excuse for you to try it. Besides; no one else deserves to have that much fun.

I quickly noticed a roughness in third gear when really cranking on it. It was driving me nuts! It would scream through first and second without missing a lick and then start to cut out upstairs in third. This only happened when I was really flogging it. It didn't appear to be fuel-related. The plugs were coloring nicely and going lighter on the secondary spring to open them earlier didn't help. In desperation, thinking it had to be ignition-related, I picked up a used Mallory dual-point distributor and hung it on there in place of the Chrysler electronic distributor. In hindsight, that was probably not a good move. (Later reasoning and performance reading/reviews would find the Chrysler spark-box probably out-performed the dual point all through the rpm range.) It helped some, but not enough. As the summer weather changed to fall, the car became more and more cantankerous to start on frosty mornings, and the roughness in third was still evident. I was getting discouraged. Winter was fast approaching, and I needed a car that would start and run to get me to work and school. Like it or not, I had to get to work. Enter the little 318...

A friend of mine knew a guy that had a freshly overhauled

318 two-barrel for sale. He'd been trying to sell it for quite some time. He also had an A-833 four-speed for sale as well. I paid a little more for the four-speed than I should have and a *lot* less for the engine than it was worth!

So the plan unfolded thusly:

Out came the 340, back on the engine stand, for head-scratching and troubleshooting purposes.

In went the little 318 with a two-barrel, Holley 500cfm on top (thrown in with the deal). I decided to hold off on the four-speed until the 340 went back in.

And, yes, I used the same come-along with the four-by-fours, if you must know.

For a "little" 318 two-barrel, the car was mighty respectable! It would light 'em up in first and second, and it ran like a house afire. This was an earlier high-compression 318; I'd say maybe a '68-'69. Anyway, it was one strong little motor.

It got me to work and college classes throughout the winter with no problems whatsoever, always started, and never lost a race.

(Pssst: I never really raced it, but nobody needs to know this... let's just keep it between friends. Well, there was this time I was coming home from work and a guy on a BSA 650 was goosing it at the lights, and I gave him a real good look at the little pissed-off tornado in between my tail lights, if that counts.)

As the winter played out, I learned some things. I learned the 318 was a strong, gutsy little motor. I learned that E60s on snow with a manual tranny and a gutsy little motor isn't the most efficient means of winter transportation. I learned about snow tires. (Remember snow tires?) I learned about mononucleosis (aka the dreaded "MONO"), and how laying on a cold garage floor when you have it can make it a much worse ordeal than it already is. At least, when I wasn't sleeping, which was, like, sixteen hours a day, I was reading, trying to figure out why the little 340 wouldn't play well with others.

In the end, it was so simple it was stupid! I'd installed

a "newfangled" AM/FM/cassette deck with the money I'd received as a high school graduation present. Naturally, the crackling of the Mallory dual point through the FM had to be dealt with, so I'd purchased a brand new set of Hi-performance, carbon core silicone ("HF Eliminating") ignition wires so I could groove to the likes of Peter Frampton and such. Anybody wanna hazard a guess as to what happens to a motor under hard acceleration with pretty high compression and under heavy acceleration (with resulting high manifold pressure, such as high gear)? Who'da thunk it?

Poof. The pistons were blowing out all the birthday candles...the HF carbon wires weren't up to the task. When the going gets tough...

In the end, that's all it was. I had this epiphany while tossing the idea around in my head during my recuperation from the dreaded "MONO." So as soon as I was better and the weather turned spring-ish, I decided to put my theory to the test by yanking the valiant little 318, bolting on the newly acquired four-speed with a brand-spanking new Hurst Competition Plus four speed linkage and dropping the 340 back into the Royal Throne Room. I put in a new set of plugs (Autolite AG-32s) with a brand-spankin' new set of 8mm *solid copper-core wires,* fired it up and stalked off to some deserted country road to test my theory.

JEEEEEEHOSAPHAT!!!!!!!!!!!!!!!!!! The thing ran like a scalded dog! Not only did the motor not miss a lick, but the four-speed made a difference like I wouldn't have believed! And wind? *Man,* I'd never seen a motor wind up that quick!

Any of you who are cat owners, or have ever owned a cat, ya know how they rub around your legs when they're hungry? And when you're half asleep, reaching for the coffee pot, there they are, rubbing around your legs. And sooner or later, you step on their paws or their tail. You know that sound? That shrieking, blood-curdling yowl? Yeah, that's what this thing sounded like when I pounced on it. Only deeper; lower. Maybe like if you had a pet panther instead of a cat.

And the cam; *Lordy,* that cam! The thing would sit at the traffic lights with this rump, rump, rumpety-rump idle, the front of the car shaking like the back end of a horse trying to get rid of a pesky fly. You could hear the compression of those pop-top pistons thudding shock waves like pealing thunder against your eardrums and smell the raw, unburned gasoline in the exhaust, and then the light would change...and there goes that pesky cat again, yowling like you broke its paw!

It was about this time a close friend let me have a slightly used Holley 650 double-pumper for the ridiculously low price of $40. (A lot of things seemed to cost $40 back then.) I bolted it on the same evening I got it and set about tuning yet another Holley.

In retrospect, it's probably a good thing my hometown (Which we did then, and shall heretofore refer to as "Mudville.") had a small police force that was spread rather thin. I never got on a first name basis with any neatly-dressed individuals in shiny black shoes, but I won't deny the opportunities were present!

I'll never forget the time I was tuning my double-pumper for full-throttle (secondary) jetting. The procedure here is to avoid breaking the tires loose off the line, do a full-power run through all four gears 'til you reach top speed (or chicken out) and then push in the clutch, kill the engine, and coast to a stop. At this point the "perpetrator" should pull a spark plug and check the coloring. White, too lean; black and sooty, too rich; tan, just right. *Sounds* simple, anyway. Of course, this is a maneuver designed for tuning on the drag strip, but not having one right around the corner, I decided a country highway would suffice. So my buddy, Jerry, and I decide we'll give it a shot, right? I turn onto this two-lane country highway, accelerate quickly up to about thirty, and then just *pound* on it! The motor is howling like a werewolf over a fresh kill, and I can feel the front end topping out the shocks trying to go airborne as I'm banging the Hurst, power shifting at 6500 between gears. I probably hit north of 100 before I chickened out and killed the motor and casually coasted to a whisper-silent stop on the shoulder. Jerry's mouth was hanging open in this disbelieving kind of look, and his glassy eyes were as big as saucers. With mock concern I asked, *"You feelin' alright, bud? You look a little peaked!"* and hopped out of the car and popped the hood. I grabbed a spark plug socket and ratchet from under the seat and had started to pull #1 plug when he emerged from the passenger side, still looking sort of dazed and confused. He then began to babble expletive praises of the little 340 while I modestly told him, "Awe, shucks, 'twarnt nuthin'..." or something to that effect. Just then a county cop coasts up behind us, lights flashing, pulls over and gets out. Oh...shit. This is *not good*. This might be *bad*, even.

"What seems to be the trouble, Son?"

(As if you didn't know. As if you didn't hear that werewolf howling on the moors mere seconds ago.)

"Uhhhh...I think I mighta fouled a plug." (gulp)

I'm sweating bullets. My hands are shaking; I almost drop the freaking plug.

"Anything I can help with?"

(Yeah, sure... let me have at least one phone call and holster your weapon?)

"Uhhhh, I think I have it fixed now officer. I'm changing the plug now."

The motor is trying to rat me out...little blue bastard!... ping, pop, ting! Tick, tick, tick. Sorta like a scorching hot frying pan when you put it in the sink...

"You sure, Son?"

(Yeah, yeah...look, just cuff me and get it over with...)

"Yessir, officer, but thanks anyway!"

He stares over the top of his aviator sunglasses for a minute, perhaps just a little too long, then walks back to the squad and sits there while I thread the (properly colored!...jetting spot on!) spark plug back in, slip on the wire, and shut the hood. Jerry shoots me an I-don't-have-bail-money look and hops in the passenger side. I start the werewolf...er, motor, and ever-so-slooooowly ease out the clutch and limp off down the road, like granny on the way home from church, nervously watching Officer Friendly in the rear view sitting on the shoulder 'til he's out of view. We shoot each other sidelong glances and both heave out this *huge* sigh of relief.

All Jerry can mutter is, "Damn! Damn you; this thing is a MONSTER!"

(You're preaching to the choir, bud!)

A Tale of Two Dusters
Chapter 3

Friends

At this point, I would be remiss if I didn't mention some of my buddies and their rides; I was not the only motorhead in Mudville.

Howard, that motor-dropping son-of-a-biscuit-maker, was actually the first to get a car; a '68 GTO with a 400. I learned some of my best chops working on that car; in fact, I damn near lived in his garage before I got my Duster. He was running a balanced and blueprinted 400, ported and polished heads with oversize valves, headers, Crane cam, Edelbrock manifold with Holley 850 double-pumper, Accell dual point distributor, and Super Coil hooked to a Muncie M22 Rock Crusher through a Borg/Warner street/strip clutch with a Mr. Gasket vertical gate shifter (Sorry Howard, but your shifter sucked compared to my Hurst.) spinning 5.13 gears. This car would top out at about 90 due to the low gearing, but man, what a ride! The "Goat" would wheel hop so violently he could've made a fortune just collecting all his friends' fillings off the floor! He "sort of" fixed it by installing ladder bars, but it didn't go away completely until he changed the gears to a more reasonable three-something.

I remember some funny Howard stories...the time when, after getting the engine installed after the build, while installing the manifold and carb (which were the last things to go on except for the distributor), he was spinning on the nuts and lock washers for the carb base. One of the rear nuts wouldn't start properly (cross-threaded) so he backed it off, and...

Yep, right down the ol' distributor hole. Down the well, like little Jessica, so to speak. It sounded somewhat like a pinball game; bouncing and ricochetting down into the bowels of that motor until we heard the dreaded hollow "thunk" of a rogue nut hitting the bottom of an empty oil pan, the kind of sound a prison door makes when it slams shut on an inmate sentenced to three consecutive life terms. We just stared at each other in disbelief, and then Howard lets out this long, drawn-out "FUUUUUDGE!" Just like Ralphie in *A Christmas Story*, only Howard didn't say "fudge" either! He fished with a magnet for hours to no avail; eventually the engine came back out and the oil pan came off, the nut sitting there cheerily in its empty metal swimming pool waiting for the fire trucks to come and fill 'er up. "Oh, hullo! Fancy meeting you here!" I learned about stuffing rags in open holes from that; I still do it today. That's a sound forever etched in my memory, and once is enough.

When we finally got the engine back in again, removed the rag cleverly placed in the distributor hole (Wonder where we came up with that one.), and fired it up, (It, like mine to follow, also lit immediately. What can I say? We were good!), while this dragon was roaring and belching fire through open headers, we could hear this distinct banging from deep within the bowels of the motor. We tried everything you could think of to find the source: push rods, rocker arms, etc. It wasn't evident 'til we pulled the distributor and saw a nice new shiny wear mark on the shaft. The boneheads who had balanced the crank had drilled holes in the counterweights and added Mallory metal to balance it; it protruded too far. End result: the engine came out yet again, and the crank had to go back for warranty work! Howard was not a whole lotta fun to be around that particular week. In the end, this was one quick Pontiac!

Then there was Dave, with his '68 396 Chevelle SS. He never pulled the motor but had the heads done, cam, manifold, Hooker headers, Holley 780 strapped to a Turbo Hydromatic 350. I don't believe he could've taken either my car or Howard's in the quarter-mile, but I had never seen a motor with so much mid-range torque when he put the screws to it! So much, in fact, that it chewed up the 350 and ate it for breakfast—Alumin-Os! The tranny case was non-repairable, so he put in a shift-kitted, Turbo Hydramatic 400. This thing would lurch so hard when he had his foot in it that it would've snapped your head off like a G.I. Joe in the hands of your bratty little nephew if it wasn't for the high-back buckets seats! I'll tell you what; at 30 mph, when he'd stomp on it, there wasn't a car we knew of that could stay with him between 30 and 60. He would literally have to ease off the gas because the tires would break loose and start smoking at 30 mph!

Jerry had a '68 Camaro RS with a 327 2-barrel—nothing to write home about there. We threw a Holley 600 and manifold on it, but, without a decent cam and exhaust to give it some lung-power, it actually was slower! He later bought an early '70s Chevelle SS 350 with cowl induction; this would've been worth a few bucks today if he still had it. It was bone-stock, and not all that quick compared to what we were used to. Bodyman Mike had a Vega. I will not dwell on this. Fellow Mopar freak Mike T. had a project '66 Barracuda fastback. I don't believe he ever finished it.

Other fellow Mopar freaks Bob and Dale had, respectively, a late-model 318 Charger and Dale, first a Demon 340 followed by a '73 'Cuda 340. Both of Dale's were bone-stock, but surprisingly quick.

There were others, of course, but these were the ones that helped either directly (such as Howard "helping" me drop my fresh motor) or indirectly (through advice, ideas, etc).

OK, enough of that "brand-X" crap. Back to the only "Motor that Matters"—MOPAR.

The old Duster was garnering quite a reputation around town, both by those who knew me, and by those who didn't... yet. Remember, the car was not yet wearing new colors and I was still cruisin' around with a blue deck lid, orange hood (I'd put it back on by then), and primer-gray left quarter and Bondo repairs. My dad referred to it as my "Navajo Cadillac." I referred to it as my Joseph Car (with it's "Coat of Many Colors"). Anyway, it didn't resemble any of the museum-quality muscle cars that occasionally graced the streets of Mudville.

Mind you, I didn't deliberately go out looking for trouble. I just stumbled across it randomly most of the time.

Like the time I was out just wasting fossil fuel. I pulled up to the traffic lights heading out of town on a four-lane highway. It was a hot June night and the windows were down; I could smell the fuel-laden exhaust and feel the exhaust thudding in my ears. The Hurst was chattering away merrily and the hood was shaking like a dog that just ambled out of a country pond, the streetlights wiggling their reflection in limpid pools on the hood as if trying to jump off. I just happened to be outside of our favorite restaurant, Dale's Coffee shop, where we motorheads hung out. There I was, minding my own business at the red light, when a brand-new Trans-Am pulled up in the right lane. There were two guys and two girls in the car. Obviously, the guys were trying to impress the girls; maybe fishing for prom dates. They had the T-tops off and all the windows down, and the radio was blasting some typical late-seventies music—R.E.O. Speedwagon comes to mind—and these guys are hootin' and hollerin' at the old Navajo Caddy (I still prefer Joseph). That didn't bother me too much. Then the moron goes and starts revvin' his Big Bad 6.6L—outside my hangout, with who-knows-who inside looking out! Well, frankly, brother...that pissed me off. I paid no attention and stared straight ahead, but my eyes were glued the opposite set of lights. Lordy, this is the longest light I've ever sat through. And then it goes yellow. Every muscle was tensed, right hand on the Hurst T-handle, the tip of my toes poised like a tiger crouched and ready to pounce while these dope-smoking punks were laughing and carrying on with no freakin' idea of what was gonna go down here.

The opposite light turned red a split-second before ours went green, but I saw it. Dinkweed next to me got caught with his trousers down in the middle of one of his looong, obnoxious revs. I dumped the clutch and put my foot in it so hard I thought it might punch clear through the floorboard. The E-60s let out a howl like the Hound of the Baskervilles and started rolling smoke while the rear end of the car slid left across the double yellow. 6500 Rpm, I slammed second and pounced on it again. Both rears lit up again and the rear swung to the right, in front of the Super Chicken, which was by now, at least 6 car-lengths behind me. I banged third hard and the rear end swung back to the left again; the little motor was talkin' the talk and walkin' the walk now, yowling like a wildcat with his hind foot caught in a blender. The noise was deafening. I really hit my stride with fourth, probably tipping 90 in a 30 zone. As I rounded a gentle curve and glanced back in the rear-view, the Thunder Chicken's headlights shown waaaaaayyyy back there—maybe an eighth mile or so—as I rounded the curve and throttled 'er back to a "reasonable" 70 mph. It was great to be alive! The motor was thrumming out its testosterone-laden song and galloping like a thoroughbred who has just outrun the entire field and has settled into his pace; a true, untamed, wild stallion. I could smell the night smell and fresh-mown grass and I reached over and popped in a cassette; Eagles, *On The Border,* and Glenn Frey was belting out Tom Waits: "Well, it happened so quickly/I went lickety-splitly/Out to my old '55..." Indeed.

I guess those two guys didn't get prom dates after all.

Well, enough about my misadventures in maintaining throttle control...back to the project at hand. (I tend to get a wee bit off track at times.)

Things were moving fast, and the car was badly in need of new school clothes—literally. I'd finished my second year of college and was leaving the state for A&P tech school in the fall. Bodyman Mike and I lined up a compressor, a Binks paint gun (sorry, can't remember which model), and respirators to go with it. I bought a fiberglass Mopar Pro Comp scoop and spent way more hours than I want to talk about getting it trimmed and shaped to fit the hood, then pop-riveted it in place and blended in the fillets with "tiger hair" (chopped-up fiberglass cloth mixed with resin). It took a number of tries to get it looking just right, then I smoothed it over with filler and sandable primer. You literally could not tell this was not a one-piece—it was that good. I didn't yet cut the hole in the hood as I wanted a true "cold air" induction setup (similar to the six-pack, air cleaner setup). I then peeled off all the decals with a heat gun and razor blade and roughed up the car for final prep. We planned the shoot for a long weekend, and I spent the week before covering things in Dad's garage with plastic and removing everything that didn't need to be in there. With the car outside, I scrubbed and swept that floor until there wasn't a spot on it. Then we bought plastic sheeting and began stapling it to the joists. We built a sort of "plastic tent" around where the car would be with the delusion that the tent would: a) keep overspray in and b) keep dust out. I set up a box fan in the widow (blowing out, of course) and taped a furnace filter to it. I ran the garden hose in under the door, set up the compressor with a regulator and water trap, and then rolled in the car. We spent almost an entire day masking. We drove up to the local NAPA and picked up a gallon of primer/sealer and a gallon of NAPA's version of Mopar Tor-Red. I believe their name was "Rally Red." We planned to shoot the primer on Friday night and the color on Saturday night.

A Tale of Two Dusters
Chapter 4

The Emperor's New Clothes

Now that Ma had bought all these new school clothes, it was time to try 'em on then send Junior off to school.

After making sure all our tape was down tight and there were no uncovered seams in the paper, I hosed down the garage floor and the sides of the "tent"with the garden hose, and then rolled the "Navvy Caddy" in. We mixed the primer up, fired up the compressor, and switched on the fan. The prime coat went on unceremoniously, without a hitch; for the first time since I owned it, the car was all one color! We slapped our high-fives and went out to the Dale's Coffee Shop, leaving the prime coat to set up overnight.

Saturday dawned clear and HOT. We'd decided to shoot the color that evening, after it had cooled off. We spent the afternoon hosing the gray dust off the floor and tacking the car to remove any loose overspray. Darkness fell, but not the mercury. I remember to this day how blistering hot it felt in the garage that night. It was now or never.

Mike mixed the paint, an acrylic enamel with some sort of gloss hardener in it. We donned respirators and doo-rags, and, looking like some freakshow scuba divers, got down to business. My job was to hold the air hose away from Mike and the paint and fill the gun cups. Mike's job was to shoot color. We laid down a tack coat and right away ran into a problem. The walls of the "tent" wouldn't stay put because the fan was exhausting so much air with the garage door cracked. We looked for small, heavy objects to anchor the plastic, but finding few volunteers, we made prisoners-of-war of numerous unwilling objects and placed them around the perimeter of the "tent" like some bizarre sentries. All better now, Mike shot the first coat of color.

Even with one coat of color, the car looked stunning. We popped out for a breath of fresh air and high-fived each other at my mom's picnic table. After a brief breather and a couple of ice-cold Special Exports, we went back in for coat number two. Coat two took longer for some reason, and by the time we emerged, the Special Xs and the paint fumes were working together in an evil medley of toxic proportions. Our eyes were burning and we might as well have not been wearing any respirators at all. We were blown, and *not* from the Exports. We shot the third and final coat in a paint-induced mental haze. It went on fairly quickly, and then suddenly we were done! We stood back admiring this lucid, gorgeous, liquid red paint when all of a sudden Mike goes, "Oh, shit! The flies!"

The flies, indeed. We hadn't counted on visitors. They'd come drifting in under the door and cruised around under the fluorescent lights which were strategically placed on the joists over the car; so we could see, naturally! They were taking in a snootful of paint fumes, then getting higher than we were from the fumes, doin' the Kamikazi Bop into that rather large, red swimming pool of fresh paint! The first one to go was flopping around like a beached walrus and Mike's going, "The tweezers! Get the tweezers!" and I'm rummaging frantically through the tool box like a wino rooting around for his last bottle. Finally I find them.

Mike reaches over the roof and extracts the flapping red walrus, which leaves a tiny little red walrus crater above the passenger side. He flings it to the floor and turns it into a permanent Rally Red streak on the concrete, and then...

...The second wave attacks. This is like Pearl Harbor! The Battle of Midway on a Saturday night! Three more Kamikazis sacrifice themselves for the emperor, leaving tiny walrus-craters in their wake! Mike and I are frantically trying to pick them out and convert them to Red Streaks before the paint stops flowing and sets up. After the fifth one Mike says, "We'd better stop...let 'em set up and we'll buff 'em out."

BUFF "EM OUT????!!!! RED WALRUSES? ARE YOU FRICKING NUTS?

That did it. The evil medley had us out of our minds—Mike EXPLODED with laughter, and, then, so did I. We had to leave the garage. We barely made it to the picnic table outside the garage before we collapsed in gales of hysterics. Mike was laughing so hard I thought he'd pee his pants. (Maybe he did.) He was slapping the picnic table with his hand and laughing so hard he couldn't catch his breath. I was, too. I guess it really wasn't that funny, but at the time...well, you hadda be there. We had tears streaming down our faces and my stomach hurt so bad from laughing I could barely walk. I went in...er...*crawled* in to get us a couple more Xs, and as soon as I came out on the stoop Mike started in all over again. Here we are, laughing like a couple of retarded loons at midnight at a picnic table while red-walrus Kamikazis were floundering around in our precious paint job. It was too funny. I'm surprised the neighbors didn't call the cops.

We finally got our act together enough to clean up the paint gun and shut down the garage for the night. The red walruses left in the pool had obviously drowned and were no longer flopping. Mike gets an epiphany and says, "We should shut the lights off...maybe the flies will go away." Duh! Had we done this half an hour ago, maybe a few of the Kamikazis would've gone back to the carrier in shame. Hindsight is 20/20, however.

I woke the next morning with the worst headache I'd ever had—not the kind of headache three beers gives you. The evil medley had done a number on us. I didn't crawl out of bed 'til noon, and that was because I couldn't stand it any more. I *had* to see what the car looked like and what damage the Emperor's Finest had done. (I kept hearing John Wayne going, "Let's see what our little yellow friends are up to.")

Mike showed up, slightly the worse for wear, complaining of the worst headache he'd ever had. Funny how I could relate to that.

We rolled it out in the daylight in all it's glory to remove the paper and tape. It was GORGEOUS! (with the exception of the "battle damage"). In the end, Mike was right. The flies just kinda flaked away under your fingernail leaving almost imperceptible bumps. Once we'd flaked them off of there we couldn't even find them. You could, however, see the craters from the few we removed with the tweezers if you looked hard; kind of like a tiny fish-eye.

Who cares? The car looked even better than I'd ever dreamed possible. There was one tiny sag in the paint way down low on the passenger door, but the paint in general was like a red pool; no fish-eyes or anything, just this mile-deep, beautiful coat of paint.

We removed all the tape and paper and let it sit in the way-too-bright hot sunlight to cure.

Every well-dressed Duster needs matching accessories. Mine was no different. The Argent Silver wheels and trim rings got cleaned and polished. I'd ordered a complete stripe kit from the Mopar dealer, and, once the paint had cured, we mustered up enough courage to put 'em on.

We started with the back stripes first, around the tail lights and trunk lock, with the little pissed-off tornado in between, getting our feet wet with decal installation. It wasn't much different than the ones we'd installed on plastic models as kids. Those went on very well, so we moved on to the side stripes. They went on straight and all, they just had a few (OK, *more* than a few) air bubbles, which took a lot of coaxing out with a squeegee. The ones we couldn't get we popped with pins and flattened. Then came the numbers; 340 on both rear quarters! Big, bold, and telling the world this was one machine to tread lightly near. Damn, this car looked hot! I topped it all off with a new Hurst T-handle done in black suede. (They used to make them that way; I don't think I've seen one like that for twenty years or more, though.) Now it looked as good as it ran!

It was late July, and I was due to leave for tech school in a few short weeks. I made the best of it, cruisin' the local scene on those hot summer nights. I was in car heaven! Little did I know the dream was about to be shattered in a few short weeks.

A Tale of Two Dusters
Chapter 5

The Journey

The summer had gone quickly; much too quickly for me, and it was time to leave for tech school, an eighteen-month AMT (Aviation Maintenance Technician) school in Tulsa, Oklahoma. This was around the middle of August, I believe. I loaded up as many tools and spare Mopar parts as I could fit in the trunk; nuts, bolts, gaskets, etc; stuff I'd never use but I took it anyway. I was following my dad, who was driving his big Jimmy half-ton pickup with the big stuff, clothes, sheets, and towels; you know. The Duster actually got fairly decent highway mileage (for that Jimmy Carter era), although that was not a huge concern; gas had not hit a dollar a gallon yet. You could still buy leaded premium!

I was a little concerned, as this was my first real road trip in the car. Not to worry! It ran and drove beautifully. I'd put on a new Walker dual two-and-a-quarter exhaust through Turbo Hush Thrush cans and reinstalled the original Duster chrome bullet tips; the motor still growled plenty, but it was a bit more civilized. Finally, no more eye-popper pounding headaches and ringing ears! We made St. Louis uneventfully the first day and stayed overnight at my Uncle Jim's house.

The next day we finished the trip, also without a hitch. When we left Chicago I was nervously scanning the gauges all the time, ear cocked for the slightest out-of-sorts sound, and fully expecting it. The second day I relaxed, finally, and enjoyed the ride. When we hit the Oklahoma Will Rogers turnpike, Dad really kicked it into high gear and smoked along about eighty (This was in the Carter-era when 55 meant 55!) with me 'drafting' along right on his tail. The Little Red Rocket fell into a kind of groove; the motor thrumming out its muscle melody, wind in my face through the open window, groovin' to Frampton, Robin Trower, and Jeff Beck. That was a ride that coulda gone on forever, but all good things must come to an end, and so it did.

Tulsa, Oklahoma—hot, dry, dusty, and flat. We stayed in a motel that first night, I couldn't say where, then the next day went down to the school and got me registered. Placement hooked me up with some student housing (a mobile home, for cryin' out loud; I was feeling more like a redneck every day!) and a "phantom" roommate, who had not yet shown up. With that all taken care of, we drove out to the fancy new digs and unloaded. We went and got a bite for lunch, then Dad drove off into the sunset.

I spent an hour or so getting unpacked, then walked outside to view the surroundings. Nothing had changed; it was still hot, dry, dusty and flat. The sun was hanging up in the sky like this blazing blowtorch; I could hear half a hundred air conditioners humming; having a battle of the bands with the locusts (Who won; they were louder when they put their insipid little minds to it.) and traffic moving past on the road. Other than that it was like a Twilight Zone episode—no wind and no people! I suppose they were all inside in the AC doing what trailer people do best, whatever that might be.

This was not a student-only mobile home park; in fact, most of the people living there were just ordinary...well, hillbillies—"Trailer trash," if you will, for lack of a better word. Now don't get me wrong; lots of the people in that mobile home park would probably give you the shirt off their back if you needed it; that's just the way they were. But I really didn't associate much with the ones who weren't students; there just wasn't time.

Being a student (cheap) on a fixed budget (cheap) with no job yet (cheap) I chose to forego the AC and opened all the windows, hoping for a wisp of a breeze; no such luck! You hear stories about illegal immigrants dying in a boxcar; well baby, I had my very own boxcar! It was like the hothouse in "Cool Hand Luke!" I took off my shirt and found myself sticking to the "pleather" love seat in the living room (if you could call it that). Three hours later and I was already lonesome and homesick and bored. I had no phone yet and didn't know where any pay phones were anyway. It was hotter than the bore of an M-16 in a fire-fight, and I decided to go find a hamburger and later, a pay phone, to call my girl back home.

Now this trailer park...er...MHP, was about two miles from the middle of nowhere. I had to drive several miles to get to anything resembling civilization. The funny thing was, there was a four-lane paved road leading there. With nobody on it! It seemed like a good place to romp on it.

I walked out onto the porch of the trai...er...mobile home, and the sun was just hanging there, this huge pumpkin-orange orb in a cloudless, windless sky. Hot as the inside of the MH was, the heat outside was like a wall you ran into; it took effort just to move into it. The seats of the Red Rocket were so hot I had to throw a blanket over them, even at six in the evening. I rolled down all the windows and popped the rears open (one of the cool features about a Duster; rear windows that work like vents), and headed out for a burger.

Naturally, I romped on it. Even in the sizzling heat she ran like a fresh quarterhorse. This was more like it! At seventy, the wind moving through the car felt like a cold shower. I pulled into this drive-in restaurant and ordered up dinner, enjoying the AC indoors. These two guys in a nice Z-28 pulled up and were admiring the Rocket outside before coming in. They asked me if that was my car (Duh, I'm the only one in here.) and we started talking cars. I told 'em I was new to town, and they're like; "Duuude! You've gotta go down on (something or other) street! Every weekend there's like this unofficial car show; some really cool stuff!" I made a mental note of it, thanked them, and finished my burger.

Right outside, as luck would have it, was a pay phone. Let me tell ya, a quarter didn't get you very far even then, despite what all the old-timers blowing smoke up your caboose tell you! I called my sweetie but ran out of quarters much too soon and found myself alone again, feeling all the worse. Well, the best thing when you're feeling blue is to...

Romp on it.

I did.

The sun was down below the horizon now; the light rapidly dying and the sweet smell of freshly-mown grass came skating in on the cooler night air. Robin Trower was goin' on and on about some funky Bridge of Sighs and the little motor was talkin' to me, daring me to put my foot in it and snarling at me when I did, and life was just a little bit OK again.

A Tale of Two Dusters
Chapter 6

School Daze

The boredom and loneliness were rapidly replaced with a whirlwind of frantic activity come Monday. Classes began, and we started off swimming in the deep end right from the get-go. I met my roommate; I'll call him "Al." (Some names have been changed to protect the guilty.) Al was a rather out-of-shape, dumpy individual with more pimples than a prom dance. He rather resembled a pepperoni pizza perched on top of a giant ground sloth. He was not the sharpest tool in the shed; in fact, you'd be hard-pressed to draw blood with this guy! His level of intelligence was fitting with the ground sloth image as well; more on this later. He was a nice guy and all, but...

I gave him half the "mobile home." I took the other half (with the "master bedroom'"if there *is* such a thing in a mobile home!) First come, first served, right? I was there first so I got dibs. Two hundred dollars a month rent; we split it down the middle. Of course, neither of us had a job, so it didn't mean diddly squat anyway. I'd payed my first month's rent and the security deposit, so he owed me a hundred bucks. That gave me about thirty days to find a job.

School was tough. Eight hours a day, half classroom and the other half shop. Homework every night. Every Friday was "quiz day," where everything you had learned that week was put to the test. Each section was either two or four weeks long, with a final exam at the end of each section. You needed a 70% or better on both the quizzes and exam to move on to the next section, or you were doomed to repeat it. This put an enormous amount of pressure on all of us. Fridays became the do-or-die day for all of us, especially on The Big Test Friday.

Naturally, this made me want to run out and find a job to fill my nanoseconds of not having something to do, but my little 340 was a thirsty little bugger and my bank account was dwindling fast, so reluctantly I started looking.

Within the first week of class I hooked up with a bunch of car guys. One of them was rooming in the spare bedroom of a little old lady with lots of house rules that he didn't think a hell of a lot of, and bunking on our sofa sounded better to him than abiding by the rules (such as lights out by 10:00 PM, no music, etc.) Splitting the rent three ways sounded OK to us as well. I'll call this guy "Dave." Dave was nuts—no two ways about it. He drove a nice, old, aqua-green '68 Impala that had no rust or anything, 327 two-barrel motor. Al bought himself a car as well; it was a big old four-door boat; an Oldsmobile 88, I think. Sometimes we'd all leave for school at the same time. We'd be jinking and feinting on that four-lane ribbon of concrete, then I'd get bored with it and wail on the little motor and it was like, "See ya!"

I found a job first, at some dinky little penny-ante grocery store. My immediate impression of the manager was that he was a bitter little toad that hated life and the fact that he was managing a grocery store staffed by youthful kids who had no intentions of making the same mistake. He barked out orders like Hitler's little love child, and I took an immediate dislike to him. But a job was a job, and I kept my mouth shut and my opinions to myself.

If memory serves me correctly, I started work on a Wednesday evening, after school. The store closed at nine. By the time we cleaned up and closed it was ten. Do the math! That left about two hours to drive home, shove something in the ol' pie-hole, and hit the books with a vengeance. I worked Wednesday, Thursday, and Friday. I'd done well on the quiz Friday, and, after work that evening, Dave, Al, and I decided to have a few beers and relax. I had to work Saturday as well.

Except Dave had been busy drinking most of the beers while I was working, which sorta pissed me off, since I'd bought it, but hey, what're roomies for, if not to take your stuff? So after a couple beers, I realized we were on "empty" and volunteered to light off the Rocket and orbit myself down to the U-Totem and pick up another twelve. Now, the U-Totem was on Pine Street, just down the street from the school, which was several miles away. This left me no option but to romp on it, as the traffic at 10:00 was nonexistent. What a cruise! It was late September, the damp, cool night air felt good for the soul, The car was running like a raped ape; what more could one want? I made the U-Totem in record time, picked up a twelve of the nasty 3.2 swill that Okies passed off as beer in convenience stores (You could only buy "real" beer (5%) in "drinking establishments" or liquor stores.) and headed home; Jeff Beck doin' the Freeway Jam from the back seat. The Little Red Minx was teasing me again, taunting me to drop the hammer. I didn't need to be coaxed. I turned left onto Mingo Road, home of the famous mobile home park, and let the horses run free!

And run they did, probably leaving a good six feet of rubber hoofprints in their wake. I throttled 'er back to about 65 and leaned back in the seat, my left hand loosely gripping the wheel, and my right palm draped over the trembling Hurst, my fingers feeling where the suede covering had worn through to the cool metal underneath. This was not a car, this was a living, breathing thing I had created and it was talking to me, singing Songs of Thunder and responding to the slightest pressure of my right toes the way a champion racehorse responds to its jockey. We were in tune, baby, carrying on a conversation in Metalspeak and she was hanging on my every word. There was not a better car in the world—ever. I was sure of it!

A Tale of Two Dusters
Chapter 7

Journey's End

In the days we sweat it out on the streets of runaway American dreams. At night we drive through mansions of glory in suicide machines.

Bruce Springsteen, "Born To Run"

Here was the turnoff into the mobile home park. I down-shifted to third, and then the Li'l Red Minx whispered in my ear.

"You don't have to go back just yet."

Well, I was thinking, "The guys *are* waiting."

The two beers spoke up, "*They drank up your beers. Let 'em wait!*"

Two Beers had a point. Still...

"It's a cool September night. You worked hard today. What's your hurry?" taunted the Li'l Red Minx.

Two Beers chimed in, *"Yeah, romp on it!"*

"Uhh...OK. If you insist."

I blew by the Mobile Home Park at 60 and found fourth again. Or shall I say, it found me.

A short distance ahead, Mingo narrowed from four lanes to two. I eased over into the left lane. A little further down was in intersection with another two lane highway. I thought about hanging a Leroy (left) at the intersection, and then the Minx spoke up again.

"Why don't you check out what's straight ahead?"

That was a kind of stupid question for a Li'l Red Minx, or anybody else to be asking; what lay ahead was a two-lane, gravel road that went to...well, who knows where?

"No sense of adventure?" taunted Two Beers.

"Shut your pie-hole. I'll go where I damn well please."

I went straight.

This tendency was to rear its ugly head again recently when I resumed riding street bikes. It's like mind-control; bending spoons and what-not. You see the intersection; your conscious mind says, *"We turn left here, to go home,"* and the bike says, *"The hell you say!"* and blows right on through and you wind up in lower North Fork, Idaho when all you were doing was going for a quick ride.

Try explaining *that* to your wife.

Anyway, it was obvious the Minx was driving now, not me. Now, class, does anyone know what happens when tarmac meets gravel at 65 mph?

Two Beers spoke up from the back of the class, *"Loss of traction?"*

Teacher: *"EXCESSIVE loss of traction."*

Ever been on a Tilt-A-Whirl? Well, that's kinda like what I was feeling. Frantically I countersteered the fishtailing rear end; first one way, then the other. The Minx was nowhere to be found; She'd punched the "EJECT" button, and I was driving again. Two Beers was uncharacteristically quiet.

Bumps, jars, a large crunching sound like a pile of books dropped on concrete, and then...

Silence.

A Tale of Two Dusters
Chapter 8

Funeral for a Friend

...You were too fast to live; too young to die. Bye Bye.
Eagles, "James Dean" (*On The Border*)

Gradually, like waking up on a Saturday morning after sleeping in, I became aware of my surroundings. I don't really think I was out, perhaps just in shock. Anyway, the first thing I noticed was that I was alive and not in a lot of pain. That was a Good Thing. The second thing I noticed was that I couldn't see a damn thing; my glasses were gone. It was unearthly quiet; like when you're sitting in the woods and suddenly become aware of a cacophony of noises in the background that were really there all along. I became aware of the hissing of a ruptured radiator, mortally skewered like a jousting knight who has just received his comeuppance. I could smell the sweet smell of glycol and taste it in the clouds of steam that drifted in through the driver's window, which had disappeared as if by magic. Hell, I could *see* the steam in the glare from the one remaining headlight, which glared out at the treetops in a fantastically absurd angle, a mortally wounded cyclops on its deathbed. I reached over and switched off the lights.

The door didn't open at first. Once, twice, three times with my shoulder, and it grudgingly popped open. Gingerly, I unbuckled the lap belt and stepped out of the car.

The engine was pinging and ticking, shedding the heat from its death-gauntlet like a mortally wounded animal, green blood pooling beneath it. In the full moon's light I could see the huge buckle in the hood. The scoop I'd labored so hard on was cracked and peeled back. It was then I noticed the telephone pole leaning crazily to one side, wires drooping low like the clothesline of a fat man, loaded with wet laundry. Things were not looking so hot at the moment.

I reached back inside and blindly rummaged around in the glovebox for my flashlight. Finding it, I switched it on and searched for my missing glasses. I finally found them, twisted and bent, between the passenger door and the seat, on the floor. They'd hit the windshield and cracked it on the way to their new burrow. I twisted and bent them enough to make them somewhat fit. Then I surveyed the damage.

It was a mortal wound; you could just tell. Like in the movies when the medic tells the sarge, "Awe, it's just a scratch; you'll be up and around in no time!"

You can't BS the old sarge. "Tell my wife...(whatever)... and hug little Timmy for me..." Then he sighs, closes his eyes, and rolls his head. You couldn't BS me either. If this was a quarterhorse, I'd be tenderly pressing the muzzle of my .44 against her head. They shoot horses, don't they?

I spied the unopened refreshments in the back seat. Well, they were unopened up to this point. I sat down in the ditch on the wet, dewy grass and popped one open.

Two Beers appeared out of nowhere. *"Hell of a thing, eh?"*

"Shove off, mate."

"Suit yourself."

Alone again, I polished off the beer, chucked the can in the ditch and opened another. And then I did what any other full-grown, testosterone-stoked, musclecar-building Sonofabiscuitmaker would do...I broke down and sobbed like a freakin' baby.

> *Once you've hit rock bottom, there's no where to go but up.*
>
> Unknown

A lot of things happened over the next forty-eight hours, but most of it was a blur. Call it shock; call it trauma; just don't call it late for dinner. Two guys stopped to see if anyone was hurt when they saw the Li'l Red Minx smoochin' with the telephone pole. I think they gave me a lift home. I say "think" because I just don't know for sure. Anyway, I got there. I must've looked a mess; bent-up specs, shiner in the works, blood oozing from various cuts, and contusions and all. And no car. Either Dave or Al (or both) drove me to the ER to be checked out. I had a shiner under construction, bruised ribs, a huge purple welt across my abdomen (from the seat belt) and a lacerated kidney, along with other miscellaneous cuts and bruises, but I was intact, at least. They released me sometime during the wee hours of the morning with a doctor's note to stay off my feet a few days, although he released me to return to school Monday. After a few restless hours of tossing and turning, I woke early to call in to work. Old Mr. Toad was most understanding; if I may quote him: *"I hired you because*

I thought you were reliable, obviously you're not. Don't bother returning." And you thought you had a nice boss! Thanks Boss; I love you, too!

At least I got to sleep in.

Somehow I managed to get the car towed back to the MHP. I got a real good look at it in the daylight. They say everything looks better in the light of day. They were wrong. This car was toast. The radiator had been cored like an apple, the motor pushed back into the firewall. The brand-new (and absurdly expensive) Mallory distributor cap was cracked and broken, looking like some absurd dead octopus with its black silicone 8mm tentacles splayed out across the top of the motor. The distributor shaft was bent. The Kustom Headers were "headed" for the scrap heap, the tubes twisted and mangled and flattened closed. The right front wheel twisted out at a grotesque angle; I crawled under to check it and saw the tie rod sleeve was broken clean in two, leaving the wheel to flop about like a hand on a broken wrist. It was then that I saw the unibody rails were twisted and bent and I knew it was game over. I actually got a couple quotes over the next couple weeks, the cheapest of which was twenty-five hundred; this just to make it driveable again. With no job and $300 as my life savings, it may as well have been twenty-five million. I began buying *Auto Traders* and looking for a suitable transplant patient, preferably an A-body.

> "Dr. Frankenstein, I presume?"
> "It's Fraaaahnkenschteen"
>
> Gene Wilder, *Young Frankenstein*

I found another job within the week and got Dave to cart me around to work and school for gas money. I knew I had to find another car, and fast. I answered an ad in the *Auto Trader* for a '71 Duster and went to look at it. It was a piece of work. The owner was a piece of work, as well. It was ugly, gold, rusty, and *ugly*—a real CrackerJack prize. It had a worn out, smoking, wheezing 318 with an auto trans (which I didn't want), butt-ugly bench seats that were all duct-taped, filthy carpeting, and an 8-track, to add insult to injury. It would've been like transplanting the heart of a young, vibrant football player into a doddering old man with one foot in the grave. He wanted me to buy it in the worst way—practically pleading with me. He'd come down a couple hundred bucks. He'd throw in his stack of old Mopar magazines and greasy old hat... excuse me while I puke...

There, that's a little better...

As much as I wanted a car, I did *not* want that one. It was just waaaaay too much work. I told him I'd think about it and made the mistake of giving him my number. He must've called three times a day for the next two weeks, until I finally told him I'd found another car just so he'd leave me alone. I could've sworn I heard him stifle a sob as he hung up the phone. I kept looking.

Several extremely disappointing days later, I was almost getting desperate enough to call him and tell him the deal I'd had fell through. Everything I looked at were rolling scrap heaps; and overpriced, to boot.

I was starting to search outside of the A-body box, looking for 'Cudas and Challengers, but nothing doing. Everything I saw was worthless or too expensive, or both.

It was October now, and the frost was on the pumpkin (or would be soon). The days were shorter and the nights cooler. The trees had begun to change, showing their brilliant hues of scarlet, yellow, and brown. Winter was coming; not yet here, but ambling down the road toward us, anyway. I knew I had to do something with the Incredible Hulk out in front, but the landlady beat me to the punch. I went in to pay October's rent and she backed me into a corner...

"Say, when ya gonna get rid of that car?"

Say, when ya gonna brush your teeth, lady...yuck!

"Ummm, real soon."

"Have it gone by this weekend or I'll have it towed and give you the bill!"

Zieg Heil, Mein Fuhrer.

I got right to work on it. I stripped that car like a coyote working a deer carcass. I took off everything—doors, fenders, rear end, seats, headliner—*headliner,* for Pete's sake! If it came off, I took it off. If it didn't, I tried. I snuck around back of the trailer and removed a handful of the five-sixteenths cap screws and peeled the yellow sheet metal back like a rotten banana and stuffed all the large parts under the trailer, safe from Broom Hilda's prying eyes. The smaller stuff I boxed up and stacked in my room.

I rented a cherry picker and pulled the motor. I'd found a storage unit nearby big enough to shoehorn it into and keep it out of the elements—heated storage, no less! One of the guys from school hauled it and the cherry picker down there and we stuffed it in there like a fat foot in a too-small shoe. Aside from the Mallory, everything else looked intact.

And the search went on...

It was a Saturday, I think. Dave had gotten a notice in the mail that there was a care package from home waiting for him at the post office. I had to work that morning and he picked me up from work; we headed out to find the Post Office. It was way the hell across town somewhere; we had no idea. We'd stopped to ask directions probably three times and been given three different answers. You gotta understand Okie to translate; *"Fust ya go dayown theyahh, then make a raaaat..."* We knew what the address was, just not how to get to the road. After about an hour of driving in circles we finally found it. Dave picked up his package and we headed back. We immediately got lost again in some sprawling subdivision full of ticky-tacky, boxy, look-alike prefab homes. Dave made a right turn into a cul-de-sac to turn around, when...

"STOP THE CAR!!!!!!!!!!!"

He slammed on the brakes; panicky, confused, and looking for a three-year-old on a tricycle in the street. Seeing none, he turned to ask me what the hell I thought I was doing, but I was already out of the car and in the street.

There, in one of the nameless, mundane, look-alike driveways of the subdivision of ticky-tacky homes sat the Holy Grail of Mopar, sunning itself under a brilliant, robin's-egg-blue sky that was so bright it hurt your eyes.

A Tale of Two Dusters
Chapter 9

The Holy Grail

The sun danced off the silver-blue finish; blinding spears of sunlight shooting off the Argent Silver wheels with their brushed-aluminum trim rings. At that particular moment I saw it; it sucked the breath from my lungs.

I was all over it.

Peering through the windows, I saw a nicely kept black vinyl interior with high-backed buckets and a manual tranny. The top of the hood and fenders had been blacked out, save for the narrow wedge down the center of the hood, the black on the fenders continuing back along the tops of the door skins and curving around the rear windows like licorice candy canes. It was a nice touch. It had the '72 grille I liked so much on the Li'l Red Minx also.

Normally, this kind of activity in a stranger's driveway would get you on a first-name basis with an 870 Remington before you could say "boo." All was strangely silent, though. Not seeing anyone about, I quickly stepped up to the front door and rang the bell. Nobody answered, but I could hear a dog barking inside from deep within the bowels of the house. Trying again with no response other than *Rex Live! in Concert*, I knocked on the screen door. Finally I heard stirring from inside the house and the grating sound of a deadbolt sliding back. The door opened a few inches, and this (Native American) Indian dude poked his face into the opening between the door and the jamb, his chin resting on the still-attached security chain.

"Yeah?"

How. You sell-um motor-wagon?

"Uhhh, is this car for sale?"

Geronimo pondered a moment, blinking owlishly in the bright October sun, then unlatched the security chain and opened the door.

"Could be."

The guy was huge. Not fat, mind you; all muscle, with no shirt or shoes on and raven-black hair down to his waist.

I rather hoped he wasn't low on his quota of scalps for the week.

He stepped out onto the stoop and walked over to the car.

We walked; we talked. He popped the hood to show me the motor; I didn't need to ask if it was a 340; it was. It was old and dirty, to be sure, but at that point I wouldn't have cared if it was a slant six; Dr. Frankenstein had other ideas. Strangely enough, I noticed it was topped with a Carter AVS instead of the standard Thermo-Quad, and was dumping the spent gases through early-style, 340 hi-perf exhaust manifolds. Strange. The color of the intake and valve covers was off, too; more of a Ford Blue than Mopar. He unlocked the car and I opened the door and stepped in. I sunk down into the high-backed buckets, as they wrapped their tendrils around me, and had a strange feeling I belonged here. I worked the shifter through the gears; yup, four speed. I'd swallowed the hook now; just waiting for him to set it.

I could feel my heart pounding. I managed to croak out, *"How much?"*

Geronimo pondered a bit more. Perhaps if I offered him a peace pipe...

"Nine hundred."

Nine hundred. Geez, and I was only short six hundred! A mere bag of shells!

"How about six hundred?"

He looked at me with these unwavering coal-black eyes as if I'd just offered to buy Manhattan Island for a handful of beads...

"Nine hundred."

Right. Had he been in on the original Manhattan deal, I'd be going to school in a London suburb.

"OK; nine hundred."

It was Custer's Last Stand all over again, and I was old Yellow Hair himself. (I did have long blond hair at the time... this was getting scary.)

Now all I had to do was find six hundred bucks.

Custer never had it so good.

A Tale of Two Dusters
Chapter 10

Pennies from Heaven

"Hello, Mom?"

Now, I wasn't one to be borrowing money; I felt bad enough that Mom and Dad had forked over enough just getting me down here and set up. But this was an emergency. I needed a car; I needed *this* car, and it was there for the taking. Mom didn't even hesitate. She said she'd mail me a check—$600 worth of Gen-U-Wine American Smackers; In God We Trust, E Pluribus Unum, et al. She told me not to worry if I couldn't pay it back just now. Bless her heart. I called Geronimo and told him I'd be by tomorrow with a deposit.

I didn't sleep much that night. The next day I got Dave to run me back over, and, true to my word, forked over every last penny I owned as a deposit. Geronimo asked me if I wanted to drive the motor wagon.

Did Custer want to get the hell out of the Little Bighorn?

We kinda just drove around the block a bit; I was nervous with him in the car; I didn't want to tear into it with the rightful owner staring at me. I drove like a granny just out of rehab...past the police station.

It drove just fine.

Several days later, Mom's check arrived. I got Dave to run me to the bank and cashed it; then off to Geronimo's teepee and sealed the deal.

This felt surreal.

Dave up and left after I'd given him the OK; probably glad to have this particular monkey off his back.

I motored my way out of the subdivision, in command of my new ship, feeling on top of the world again. As I headed out toward the freeway, I had thoughts...

One of my friends believes in fate. For example, he doesn't wear a helmet when he rides. His philosophy: "If I'm meant to crash and die, there's nothing I can do to change it. So lean back and enjoy the ride."

Bullshit.

My philosophy is a bit different. I don't believe in "fate."

I also don't believe I'm some nameless organism twisting about in a faceless, cold orb of a world twirling about in outer space...

I believe in The Big Boss Upstairs.

And I am sure, in my own mind, that The Big Boss Upstairs knew exactly which road the Li'l Red Minx was taking me down, and so He grabbed me by my wide '70s lapels and shook me like one of those Jibber-Jabber dolls they used to sell.

"Wake up, fool.

"You're free to make your own choices...just make sure they don't get you killed."

They damn near did.

This was in the forefront of my mind as I rolled on the power pulling onto the freeway.

Don't get me wrong; once a motorhead, always a motorhead. You just get a little more choosy about where you pick your battles.

This looked like a good spot for a fight.

I merged with traffic, signaled left, and deftly slid her into the right lane.

Then I romped on it.

For an tired, old 340 (the odometer read 80,000 miles) this thing got up and smacked me with the whammy stick. Holy Moses! Did I say, "tired and old"? I was wide awake and paying attention now! Not the kind of smacking I'd get from the Red Rocket, but impressive nonetheless. I took a gander in the rear-view and wondered where the mosquito truck was. There was a cloud of blue smoke hanging in the air that could've only come from Yours Truly, hanging in the breeze like the smoke from a thousand campfires, and I thought of the old cartoon they used to run in the *Chicago Tribune* each fall called "Indian Summer." *"Indian Summer,"* I thought with a grin, *"Geronimo, you rascal, you."* So she burned a little oil. Oh well, I knew of this low-mileage 340 laying low in a heated storage shed somewhere...

"Dr. Frankenstein, I presume?"

340s rock.

The thrumming, hypnotic lullaby of the motor crooned to me as I cruised home.

A Tale of Two Dusters
Chapter 11

New Acquaintances

It didn't take long to get acquainted with my new friend. Oh, sure, there were limitations—like how many quarts of oil one could carry in the trunk. Seriously, though, it wasn't that bad. It really only burned a lot of oil when I romped on it. I tried to behave myself; tempered by the memory of what happened last time I threw caution to the wind; that, and the fear of heaving a rod through the side of the block on a high-time motor. Let's just say I was a little more...civil. As for the car itself, truth be told, I liked it better than the Li'l Red Minx. The interior was certainly nicer, the buckets were like sitting in a La-Z-Boy.

The car was not nearly as loud. It idled nicely and played well with others. And it was really a nice looking car; unfortunately, just not as good looking as the Li'l Red Minx had been. I was spoiled, forever tainted by that stunning red paint job.

Speaking of which, Ol' Red was long gone, hauled off to the crushing block, I presume, where old cars go to die. I tried not to think of it much. I had another car to concentrate on now, and school and work were really stepping up the pressure.

I'd left the part-time job in the store and now had a better-paying factory job. Of course, it meant more hours, and studying became more of a chore.

> *Can't we all just get along?*
>
> Rodney King

Roommates...ahhhh, what can one say about one's college roommates? I truly appreciated their support during my crisis. But one's patience has limitations.

I mentioned earlier that "Al" was not the sharpest tool in the shed. He was no dummy, intellectually, but he had absolutely no mechanical skills whatsoever. I do not exaggerate. He was skimming through the classroom sessions by the skin of his teeth, but failing every shop class. By the time he got to "Basic Hand Tools and Shop Practices," the writing was on the wall.

Now, the school policy was this: if you failed a class, having already paid for it, you were allowed to retake the class as many times as you saw fit to pass it, free of charge. Al put this policy to use beginning with Month One and faithfully followed up with every class after. By the time we were six classes into the program, Al was still stuck in class number three and failing.

Now, I ask you with all sincerity; how does someone fail *"Basic Handtools and Shop Practices" THREE TIMES???????!!!!!!!!!*

Answer: You have no mechanical skills whatsoever. But we covered that.

And this wasn't his only handicap.

He was lazy, and he was a slob.

Before you jump in here and remind me that this description matches ninety-eight percent of all college students, let me counter by saying, "You don't know Al."

First off, the guy wouldn't work. Nothing pisses you off more than being gone all day—first at school, then at work—and coming home to find your trail...er...mobile home looking like Hiroshima a week after the blast; Al with that goofy grin watching TV with dishes piled up to the ceiling from breakfast—*his* dishes, not ours—we washed ours and put them away. And since he didn't work, he never had enough money to stave off his voracious appetite, so he would descend upon my poor, innocent staples like a plague of ravenous locusts. Beer, macaroni and cheese, hot dogs; he showed no preference and no mercy. Now remember, this is the guy who resembled a giant ground sloth. He would poke that proboscis into the fridge and Hoover out anything that wasn't bolted down. One time in particular; my sweetie had sent me a Betty Crocker Instant Brownie Mix box. I followed the directions dutifully, baking the mix in the box it came in, which magically turned into a brownie pan (How do they *do* that?) and put them into the fridge to cool. By then it was oh-dark-thirty and I hit the books, and, before I knew it, it was time for lights-out. I dreamed about those freakin' brownies all night. I lusted after them all day in class the following day and at work afterwards. I walked in the front door that night with brownies on the brain. I went straight for that fridge like a shorthair on point, locked on to a big ringneck pheasant, opened it and...

No beer.

No brownies.

No Al.

The last empty beer bottle stood on its head in the overstuffed, overflowing wastebasket, right next to the empty Magic Pan.

I stormed over to his side of the MH and knocked (OK;

pummelled) on the door. He opened it, blinking owlishly with his typical shit-eating grin.

"*Where are my brownies?*" I shrieked hysterically.

"*Brownies...? Oh, yeah, yeah, I ate some. They were good.*" He added the last, as if that would somehow make me feel better; that they were good. That he'd enjoyed them. And, *some????* If he'd left me even one...

"*I'll bet they were, you freaking MORON! But then how would I know?*"

The last, fairly dripping with sarcasm.

"Geez, you don't have to get all bent out of shape."

I mumbled something about his ancestors and primates having a common thread and stormed off to bed.

Al never did laundry in addition to never doing dishes or cleaning. Maybe he thought we had a maid. Well, if we did, I never saw her. Never doing laundry meant always having dirty clothes on and the guy could really be a total assault on your olfactory sensors when it got right down to it. In the summer, the guy was positively ripe. He did manage to shower on occasion, though. Eventually, we had to have a talk with him about his bad habits. We ended up dividing the fridge into three regions; woe to he who crossed the boundaries. Dave finally got pissed enough to divvy up the dishes (which were mostly his anyway) into three separate stacks. He could never have a bowl of cereal because all the bowls would be piled up by the sink with hard, crusty cereal glued to the edges like concrete and filled with clumps of lumpy, sour milk—all Al, eating *our* cereal. For us to have cereal, one would have to wash the dishes first. I truly believe there was some devious, deep thinking behind this phenomenon.

The division of food and utensils seemed to work. Al eventually got a part-time job (finally!) to finance his junk-food monkey. This was a guy who could inhale a Super Size bag of Doritos and a gallon of milk at one sitting. This was OK, as long as they weren't *my* Doritos. This festive ritual was observed time and time again by Yours Truly. He ended up buying paper plates and bowls with plastic silverware so he could avoid doing dishes. This was fine by us as well. It kept the flies down.

Dave—now this guy was a piece of work as well. He was not a slob by any means. He did dishes, did his laundry, and kept his space neat and tidy. Dave's problem was twofold; first, he was a budding alcoholic. Second, he was insane.

Now, when I say "insane," I mean he would do things that were *just not right*. Like, we'd be eating dinner at the all-you-can-eat buffet and some couple would walk in; Dave would make some lewd or otherwise inappropriate comment towards the Better Half of this couple at Public Address Volume, which would naturally attract the Other Half's attention, who naturally had biceps as big as my thigh, perhaps on his way home from the Nautilus club or killing tigers with his bare hands at the circus.

I don't know this guy; I'm just sitting here with him. Never seen him before in my life...honest. Please don't kill me, too.

There were some close calls. And then there was the driving. That was another reason I had to have my own car. A quarter of the time he was drunk. A quarter of the time he was reckless. The other half of the time he was drunk *and* reckless.

He found a new group of friends across town that were just like him and began spending less and less time at the MH. This suited me just fine. His grades and attendance were starting to slip, and the writing was on the wall. Actually, the writing was on the fridge. One day I got home from work and found a note taped to the fridge saying he'd moved in with the cross-town boys; all his stuff was gone (including the dishes). Good riddance. I saw him occasionally at school (we were in different classes now), and remained on good terms, but I was relieved he had left. I eventually heard an (unconfirmed) rumor that he and a couple of his roomies had been expelled for having pot on campus. Whether true or not, I never saw him after that.

Later down the line, Dave's spot on the sofa was taken by "Matt." Matt was a curious individual; sort of a lanky, gangly, tall drink of water. He was OK at first; after a while he developed some peculiar peccadilloes that would chafe at me like a burr under my saddle. But at the time, he was a welcome relief from the insanity of Dave and the slothful sloppiness of Al. Matt drove an old, beat-up Ford F100 pickup. Though he was past the time of the Red Rocket, he became obsessed with my new ride and eventually bought one of his own; a sky-blue Dart with twin scoops on the hood and a 318 that had seen better days. This motor later wound up in pieces in my living room(!), the purpose of which was unknown, for some mission which I don't believe ever was accomplished. This was much too big of a project for a working student to embark upon, especially one without a clue. I have a sneaking suspicion that the mission involved having the resident Mopar King lend a hand in building the motor and put it all back together for him. I probably would have, but by that time we were barely on speaking terms. But the Mopar net flings wide, and it's not hard to envision why he would get caught in it, what with my car and magazines and all the stories and conversation. It's said that the most sincerest form of flattery is imitation...we'll just let it go at that.

Anyway, Matt and I would have long conversations late into the night involving Mopars and 340s and good stuff like that. We actually made it down to the street I mentioned earlier in this story a few times. After pondering about the name of this street for weeks now, a name finally popped into my head: Peoria Street. I'm not sure if this is correct; but that's the name that popped into my head so we'll go with it.

Tulsa was not the way I'd envisioned it; Hicksville. It was different, to be sure. Yeah, the Okies were laid back, for sure. But they were cool, too. If you were into music and guitar (I was) Tulsa was a sort of back-alley Nashville with a whole sub-culture of budding musicians and such. You'd go to a guitar store to buy a pack of strings, or browse and drool, and some guy would walk in with his wife and kid and pick up a guitar and start picking and just blow you away. And I'd be thinking, "This guy probably works in a factory and has an everyday mundane life with his family, and he could blow half my guitar heroes off the stage." And it was no big deal. The city was full of guys like that.

So it was with the car culture. Everyone was a shade-tree mechanic. Hopping-up cars was like baling hay to those people; they did it well and with little effort. And the interesting thing was, Tulsa was a Mopar Mecca back then. Oh, sure, you'd see your Bow Ties and your Found On the Road Deads, but what amazed me was the number of Mopars and the pristine condition many of them were in. This became glaringly apparent the moment we hit Peoria Street on a Saturday night.

...Beyond the Palace, hemi-powered drones scream down the boulevard. Girls comb their hair in rear-view mirrors and the boys try to look so hard...
Bruce Springsteen, "Born To Run"

This was Peoria on a Saturday night. Some of my mental snapshots: a Screaming Yellow 'Cuda with its strobed black stripes speaking volumes without saying a word; no hood and dual Holley 660s stretching for the moon on the twin mountain peaks of a tunnel ram, dual velocity stacks perched on top as if to announce to the world that this was truly a King. A Plum Crazy, hemi-powered rag top 'Cuda that might dispute His Lordship. A dynamic duo consisting of an AAR 'Cuda and a T/A Challenger parked nose-to-nose in a shallow Vee in a parking lot, their glass hoods propped up by two-by-fours and showing off their sets of triplet carbs like proud parents; both red, like two brothers, you could see the Mopar family resemblance; while the owners sipped liquid courage from long-neck bottles. The chrome. The smell of raw, unburned gasoline mingled with exhaust. The rumble and thunder. They would pace back and forth, up and down, this stretch of hot tarmac like a prowling pack of wild dogs, snarling and snapping at each other. Occasionally one would lunge at another, tires squealing, engine snarling, and the acrid smell of burned rubber would sting your nostrils. Guys were shouting at each other through open windows and laughing, music was in the air. It was hot, it was summertime in Tulsa, and young America was on the prowl.

What was truly amazing was, there were no cops. At least, I saw none. These folks seemed to know how far to push it, and no further. I saw no fights, or anything like that, just a bunch of motorheads gathered together in a common cause steeped in Sun Super 260 100+ octane gasoline (Yes, they were selling it there; at one of the gas stations on Peoria.) A big black Polara 440 rumbled down the street like an overgrown bodyguard, the big block barking out its deep rumbling thunder. Schools of Barracudas trolled up and down while Challengers sparkled and shone under the streetlights. There were Dusters, Darts ,and Demons. A white Super Bee with what appeared to be open headers would prowl up and down and then park by the T/A Brothers. After a little bit he'd get up and do it again. It was a magical place in a magical time. How could you see and experience this without being affected; without being infected?

Little wonder Matt bought the Dart.

A Tale of Two Dusters
Chapter 12

Back to the Future

But I'm getting ahead of myself. We've jumped ahead to '79 now, and the dial of the Wayback Machine is still set for 1978. Come along Sherman, and follow Mr. Peabody back where we're supposed to be—the fall of '78.

You know this had to bug me; having a potent, yet oil-guzzling motor under the hood, while the heart and soul of the Red Rocket lay slumbering quietly in a storage unit. Yeah, it did. But I needed my car on a daily basis and with the new factory job I was working, Saturdays as well. One-day engine swaps were not my forte.

So I, Dr. Frankenstein, carefully crafted a plan. I would have Dad drive down at Christmas break with the Jimmy and we'd haul the sleeping dragon back home with us; carefully, so as not to wake it.

I'd have two weeks to make the transition.

One of my teacher's favorite sayings was: "Plan your work, then work your plan."

That's how I planned it; that's what I did.

But nothing ever goes quite the way you planned, does it?

All went well the first leg of the trip. We stopped in near St. Louis to see my uncle and stayed the night. Next morning, bright and early, we hit the road again. About two hours out of Chicago we ran into snow flurries, which began to get heavier and wetter as we approached the city bypass. Darkness was coming on early, aided by the heavy clouds and falling snow blocking out the sun like a dark cloak. By the time we'd passed the city it was coming down hard; wipers and defrost on "HIGH." It was about then, during one of my gauge scans, I noticed the ammeter needle on the wrong side of the gauge.

"Crap," I thought, *"less than an hour from home and I'm shedding electrons like a dog shedding fleas in a bathtub. I'll cross my fingers, and maybe I can make it home."*

No such luck, Bonzo.

First the wipers went; slowing down to the point where I just shut 'em off. Then the defrost blower went. So now I'm driving through heavy, wet snow with no wipers or defrost, trying to follow Richard Petty in the GMC. I rolled down the window and was using my gloves inside and out to try to keep the snow off the outside and the fog off the inside—while driving. I made a valiant stab at it for a couple miles, but when the headlights started to go, I knew I was beaten.

Fortunately for me, Richard Petty noticed the headlights in the rearview.

We were now about forty-five minutes from being home

free. Dad pulled off at the Lake Forest Oasis and parked. I pulled up next to him and the engine gave one last shuddering sigh, and then gave up the ghost as the final electron in my ignition unit left the building.

There wasn't much I could do. At least the car was in a well-lit parking lot off the highway. I grabbed a crescent wrench from the glove box, popped the hood, and yanked the battery. I figured if I charged it all night, I could probably make it home tomorrow without wipers or blower. I locked the doors and we drove on home. Besides, my fingers were totally wet, frozen, and numb from wiper duty.

I was right, but just barely. The next day the front had passed, and it was brilliantly bright, without a cloud in the sky, and colder than a witch's tit. The car fired right up, all perky and rarin' to go, and after about two miles I was beginning to feel like a Popsicle. I didn't dare run the heater blower, and without the fan, let me tell you, the heater in an A-body ain't diddly-squat! I was actually sore from shivering. The car finally died at a stop sign two blocks from the house. Dad gave me a jump and I made it home; finally!

Dad had a spot cleaned out for me in the garage; the same spot where just a few months (seemed like an eternity) earlier, we'd survived Red WalrusFest/Pearl Harbor. I would've liked to go visit some of my friends and all, but there was work to be done...

I knew the drill. The four-by-fours went in their usual place, and the Zebco 404 Drop-A-Motor winch was hanging from the chain. I think I had the motor out in less than two hours. I set it on a little four-wheeled dolly and wheeled it off into a corner like a dead man on a gurney on his way to the morgue. I didn't have a sheet to cover its face. The alternator was, of course, toast. I had to search high and low to find a rebuilt; all the local auto parts stores could order them but had none in stock. There was a Farm & Fleet about twenty miles away that finally told me they had one over the phone—road trip! By the time I got back, it was cold, dark, and I wanted to see my girl. That was enough monkey business for my first day of "vacation."

The next morning, after a hurried breakfast, the Frankenstein Motor was perched in its new home long before the sun had hit its zenith. I left the mounts loose for the exhaust; what to do about the exhaust? I wasn't about to bolt up the HiPo manifolds to this motor!

But I was in sort of a pickle; I'd spent more than I'd planned on gas and that damn alternator. I still had Christmas shopping to do for my family, and for my girl as well. Headers weren't really in the budget, and the Kustoms I had previously had gone up in price considerably.

I sure as heck didn't want to ask Mom; I hadn't paid back the money I'd borrowed for the car yet. And Dad had spent a lot on gas, driving down to haul my motor up, and besides, it was Christmas. I told my sweetie that night on the phone about my concerns; she said not to worry, that I would figure something out; I always did.

Well, who should show up next morning but Santa, looking suspiciously like the girl I'd spoken to the night before. *"Ho Ho Ho! Merry Christmas!"* with a plain, unmarked box full of...HEADERS!

She'd gone up to Jim's World of Speed and knowing nothing other than "'72 Duster" and "340" had picked me up a set of Doug Thorleys. Now, that's the kind of girl you hang on to! (I did.)

I marked the duals where the collectors would go and sawed 'em off with a hacksaw and bolted up the collectors; temporarily tying it all together with muffler clamps. Things were looking up.

The next ugly little problem to rear its head involved the radiator; remember, though this was a '72 Duster, I had determined the motor to be of an earlier vintage. It was. And most of you who know Mopars know one of the changes instituted in '72 was a higher-flow water pump with the hose on the other side, which required a different timing cover, and...you know where this is going, right? I thought so.

"So," you're thinking, *"just swap the timing cover and damper and water pump and be on your way..."*

Right.

I started doing this. I had the timing cover off the "Valiant Little 318 That Could" and on the 340 before I had time to think about it. Easier done than said. I was getting set to bolt up the damper from the 318 when I saw the ominous mystic hieroglyphics scribed on the front of my 340 damper..."FOR USE WITH CAST 340 CRANK ONLY!!!!!" This was not a kindly advisory or caution note; it meant business. What it meant, in a nutshell, was *only* the damper from FrankenDuster could be used on the FrankenDuster motor. And the timing mark was in the wrong spot for this timing cover/water pump combo. Now I was stumped. Either go out and buy a different radiator,

...or...

I love mechanical problems. Especially when they kick your ass. You're beaten, humiliated, and sent home in shame. And then, you turn the tables.

Such was the case. *"What if,"* I thought, *"I reinstall the cast crank damper and realign the timing marks to the old-style timing cover using timing tape?"*

Worked like a charm. Score one for the Captain.

The only issue left to deal with was the spark-box. I mentioned that the Mallory had been sent to the scrap heap by the accident. The 340 I'd just removed had a points-type distributor. The Valiant Little 318 That Could also had a points-type distributor. But I still had the original Chrysler electronic ignition from the Red Rocket when I'd installed the Mallory. On it went. This was too easy.

Time for the moment of truth. I'd burned up my first week of vacation and was into the second. I filled the pan with oil, the radiator with Prestone, crossed my fingers, and thumbed the key...

As with the first time, it lit immediately.

Hello Old Friend, it's really good to see you once again...
Eric Clapton

Cold or not, I was in ecstasy. A few quick adjustments to timing, recheck the float height on the Holley, and we were ready for a test-hop. Though it was cold with snow on the ground, the roads were clear and the sun was out. I slid in behind the wheel and eased her out of the garage and backed slowly into the street.

It was immediately apparent that there had been some changes. Gone was the "plays-well-with-others" friendly idle. Gone was the sloppy factory tranny linkage. Gone was the pleasant exhaust rumble, exchanged for a mean, lopey growl. The transplant was a success; Dr. Frankenstein was now an evil genius pariah, forever shunned by the world, and the long-slumbering beast was awake...and voraciously hungry. I motored casually through town, past the outskirts and out onto the open road.

"Psssst...pssst!" (in my ear) *"Wanna play around?"*

It was the ghost of that pesky Li'l Red Minx...a phantom voice echoing from the past: a voice that had been eerily silent these past few months.

Go away.

She'd gotten me in enough trouble for one lifetime. Besides, this car didn't seem, well, "minx-y"

Yet there it was.

I suppose I should tell you I behaved myself, driving like an elderly English gentleman out for a morning jaunt in his motorcar down by the white cliffs of Dover. What a great ending for a story, especially one to tell your children at bedtime! Bad boy builds fast car. Bad boy crashes fast car. Bad boy learns his lesson and drives like granny, until he's as old as granny!

Get real.

I will admit my enthusiasm was and remains tempered by the Jibber-Jabber shaking I'd gotten about the time the Li'l Red Minx made her untimely exit. Let's just say I looked further down the road and was a bit more careful about where, when, and why. But you don't keep a quarterhorse locked in a petting zoo. And like the "punk" said to Clint Eastwood, when asked the eternal question, *"Do I feel lucky today?"*

"Well...do ya...punk?"

"I gots ta know!"

I found out. Real quick.

There was something different about this car, though. It was more of a..."gunslinger," for lack of a better word.

It didn't scream, *"Race me...I'm fast!"* like the Red Rocket had.

It didn't holler, *"Sheriff; I'm-a-callin' you out!"*

No fancy cowhide vest with twin cross-draw holsters snuggling up to ornately-engraved, nickel-plated .45s with pearl handles, hundred-dollar boots, with jangly silver spurs.

No, just an ordinary dusty cowhand with his well-worn holster, lackluster wood-handled .45 with the bluing worn down to shiny metal in all the right places. One who doesn't talk much.

Ordinary.

But deadly.

And as I put my foot into it, I realized this one would put a bullet smack between your surprised, wide-as-saucer eyes before your fancy custom cross-draw muzzles ever cleared leather.

The Man Who Shot Liberty Valance...John Wayne! I was driving John Wayne!

A Tale of Two Dusters
Chapter 13

Glory Days

*Glory Days, well, they'll pass you by/Glory days, in the
wink of a young girl's eye, Glory days...*
Bruce Springsteen, "Glory Days"

I'd finished with time to spare; a day, anyway. So I got to
at least visit with a few friends for a bit. We met up at the old
hangout, Dale's Coffee Shop, to catch up on old times and for
me to once again spin the tale of the Li'l Red Minx and Two
Beers and introduce John Wayne to the boys.

The approval rating for John Wayne was about fifty
percent. Bodyman Mike, of course, was biased, as he'd done

the stunning red paint on the Red Rocket. Who could blame him?

We stayed up to the wee hours of the morning eating toasted pecan rolls and drinking coffee (which morphed to decaf sometime after midnight) and spinning tales, reminiscing about hot summer nights terrorizing the streets of Mudville and discussing our lives, our hopes and dreams, joking, and just plain shootin' the bull.

Little did we all know it would be sort of a last hurrah; never again would we find ourselves all together like this. By the time I got back from school a year later, our little group had scattered to the four winds: married, careers, raising families; dream cars parked and tarped or gone altogether to make room for the family sedan and all American that goes with it. Not necessarily a bad thing, mind you, bartering your youth for the responsibility of adulthood, rather just a part of life that everyone eventually goes through. (But at that time we were all blissfully unaware of it, though a few of my friends were already started on the journey.) Howard was already married with a baby girl; Dave as well. I would not see Dale, Bob, Mikey T., or Tom again; long since gone from Mudville to places unknown by the time I returned. But hell, we couldn't know that as we sat there drinking the steaming hot cups of brew and snacking on TPRs. Life was good. These were our Glory Days.

We talked of Trans-Ams getting their clocks cleaned; clouds of smoke billowing off some nameless obscure guy's red Duster's tires and filling the restaurant with the pungent, acrid stench of burning rubber; of nervous, sweaty-palmed conversations with balding, rotund officers of the law; of wheel-hopping GTOs and tranny-busting Chevelles. Yeah, we talked about all of that and more. And we said our goodbyes with well-intentioned promises to keep in touch and do this again, soon.

We never did. Not like that.

"...Glory Days, well, they'll pass you by..."

So I loaded up The Duke and made the long trip back; this time without escort and all in one long haul. (No stopping at my Uncle Jim's this time.) If you ask me, it was a rather ballsy move; driving a car that far that had just had an engine shoe-horned into it a few days earlier; but the trip was blissfully uneventful. I had complete faith in my own abilities and the condition of the car I was driving; this thing that I had created. Perhaps I shouldn't have, but I did; and so I just went on and did it.

Now we were out of the basics and really into the heavy-duty stuff in school. Between school and work, there was little time for anything else. Though the Tulsa winters were not really winters by Chicago standards, there wasn't much to do except study (and read car magazines). School was going well for me, so-so for Dave, and terrible for Al; he was on the verge of flunking out. Things between Dave and myself had deteriorated to the point where he moved out. Al found new hope through one of his counselors, who suggested he try NDT inspection (Non-Destructive Testing) instead of the course of study he was taking. He took to it like a duck to water. Like I said previously, he was actually a pretty sharp guy; he just had no mechanical skills. Given this new lease on life, he forged ahead, renewed.

With Dave gone, tensions eased up a bit between Al and myself. We'd laid the ground rules down, and he knew pretty much not to eat my food or leave dirty dishes. He was still stuck on the paper plate thing, which, while it made for a lot of garbage, was OK by me; we had a pretty big dumpster right around the corner. I was still struggling financially, though, and trying to find a way around it. One gets tired of Stokely/Van Camps Pork and Beans mingled with cut-up hot dogs and melted cheese five nights a week rather quickly.

The answer came to me one Saturday at work. My supervisor

was, again, complaining how another day guy had left and they needed another full-timer. I asked, just out of curiosity, how much the job paid; it was about double what I was bringing home due to the extra hours and the pay differential. And the lights came on. See, the school ran both day and night classes. If I could make the switch...

I did. And Lord, what a different world! The night school guys were, well...different. More mature, older. Married, family guys, guys with responsibilities, guys with more on their minds than floating off Mom and Dad's dollars (or Uncle Sam's V.A. bennies). It was a new crowd; a new scene. And now I was a full-time day-shift worker. Within three weeks I was a lead, then shift supervisor the following month. No more Van Camps, and at last I could actually save a little money!

It was in night school that I met "Matt." He was a decent enough guy at first. His living arrangement wasn't working out (I later was to discover why) and he assumed the sofa and a third of the rent. It sounded good at the time. About this time I also met up with "the boys," also night students. The boys consisted of Jim, Lloyd, and Dale, who had rented a house across town which became known as "The Homestead." Now, The Homestead was famous for two things: Friday Night Post-Quiz parties and car-talk. All the guys at The Homestead were big-time motorheads. After working hard all week to study and pass the tests and quizzes on Fridays, what better way to end a successful week than having a few (OK, a *lot* of) beers and talking cars? Yeah, I couldn't think of one either.

That's what we did. Well, myself and Matt, we watched what we drank rather carefully as we had about a five-mile drive home. No repeats of Mopar Minx Mania for me; thank you very much. We took turns being designated drivers long before we'd ever heard of such a thing.

But now, the boys? Well, they lived there and had nowhere to drive. This is probably a good thing, as for the most part, these guys could barely navigate to the bathroom from the kitchen on a full head of steam. (Unlike myself and Matt, they didn't have to drive home or work in the AM) I'm talking bouncing off the walls. But it was all in good fun. We talked motors and cars and school and blew off a lot of steam. Plus they had a really kickin' stereo and neighbors that didn't care. My, how we could work those speakers! The guys would get shit-faced and crank it up and start having these air-guitar contests. At least that's what they'd call it now; back then it had no proper name. I give Dale credit for inventing the whole air-guitar phenomenon. Of course, being an axe-swinger myself, I sorta had an edge on the guys, and being a bit less, shall we say, "inebriated," helped as well.

Of course, there was the occasional Friday night "Air Jam" when Matt was Designated Hitter and I didn't have to work next morning. I usually won those rare times by theatrics alone—me and Captain Jack, that is. Ooooooh; my head hurts just thinking about it. Dale was trying like hell to outdo me one of those nights and had ended this Ronnie Montrose "solo" on his knees, head flung back as if barking at the moon, with his eyes squinched closed...then he lurched up and careened off the hallway walls like they were bumpers in some grotesque pinball machine, down to the Porcelain Temple (TILT!) where he paid homage to some "Ralph" guy, at least we think he did. He kept on repeating the guy's name over and over, "RALPH!" this, and "RALPH!" that. Lloyd was laughing so hard he sprayed a mouthful of beer everywhere in a huge Budweiser shower—Lloyd, Mr. "Barracuda," the one true die-hard Mopar fanatic in the bunch beside myself—Bud foam clinging to his beard, the entire kitchen looking like a pipe bomb had detonated inside a keg. Lloyd was a big guy. Beer was dripping off the hardwood cabinets as if we were exploring deep in the bowels of a cave somewhere—"Tom Sawyer" came to mind, halfway expecting to see Injun Joe lurking around the corner. I've never regretted not having to clean up that kitchen in the morning.

Back down the hall, the homage to RALPH! had stopped and had been replaced by weak "urking" noises and the sound of a flushing toilet. After a bit, the bathroom door hinges creaked briefly, followed by the sounds of shuffling feet and of Dale's bedroom door closing, and he was seen no more that night. We didn't have the heart to bother him to tell him he'd won the contest for "Best Original Finish." That could wait 'til Monday.

But, we were talking cars, were we not? There was a guy—I'm not sure of the relationship with the boys—who had a nice Chevy II parked in the garage of the Homestead. I think the guy lived there sometimes, or maybe even owned the house, but I only saw him a few times. Martin, his name was. Anyway, this Chevy II had a real trick custom paint job with all kinds of overlapping colored lines and geometric shapes on a bright yellow base coat, and a big rectangular hole cut smack in the middle of the hood with a couple 660 Holleys poking out from atop a tunnel ram. It had a roller cam...I forget the specs now...and chrome Hooker Pro Race fender well headers (open, naturally). The one or two times Martin fired it up in that garage, the noise was absolutely deafening. One night after a few beers, Martin wanted to "show us something," so we all went out in the garage. He shut the lights off and fired this sucker up and showed us these twelve-inch rooster tails of blue flame barbecuing the garage floor—too cool! I never saw him drive it, though. Matter of fact, the car had no plates. I rather think he might have bought it on a whim. But that dog would bark, let me assure you!

Dale, now he had a Gutless...I mean, Cutlass...faded red with a 350 Olds motor. He did some work on it...put a cam in it, and an Edelbrock manifold with a 600 Holley. Thing was, he didn't know what the funny little toothpaste tube of cam lube was for so he chucked it in the gravel. He found out after about 1000 miles. Then he put another cam in it, this time with judicious use of the toothpaste, and it ran pretty strong for an otherwise stock motor. He had a huge flat spot in the acceleration curve, and we fine-tuned those secondaries to where he'd chirp 'em every time in second when he romped on it.

Lloyd had left his '66 Barracuda back in California, but had brought plenty of pictures. I swear he wrote love letters back home to the thing. It was a bit rough, as all our rides were, but he sure loved that car! He drove around a little yellow MG that was a scream. One time for a kick, we got six or seven guys in the school parking lot and picked it up where it sat between two cars and turned it sideways, then went back inside to watch. The look on his face was priceless, but he kept his cool. He turned on the stereo and kicked back and waited for the guys at either end to leave, then simply fired it up and drove off. One cool cat. He knew it was us that did it and gave us crap for weeks! With his scraggly red beard, Lloyd was a dead-ringer for Clint Eastwood in *The Outlaw Josie Wales*— only bigger.

Jim was a sandy-haired, freckly sort of guy who loved cars, especially muscle cars, but didn't own one. He just admired from a distance. Jerry, one of my buddies from Mudville, had come down to T-Town to begin flight training as a professional pilot and brought along his '72 Cowl Induction Chevelle and his sense of humor; he joined in with us and fit right in! All in all, we had plenty to talk about at the Homestead on Friday nights, believe you me!

A Tale of Two Dusters
Chapter 14

The Learning Curve

Days passed into weeks, and weeks into months. We got used to the patterns of school, even though each month was a different subject, different problems, but the approach was the same. Mondays, new topic. Tuesday, Wednesday, and Thursday, drill it into our heads. Friday, quiz. Last Friday of the month, final exam. The days, though daylight was still fairly short, in themselves were long. Six a.m., up, shower and quick breakfast. Into the Duke-mobile and off to work; start work 7 a.m. Work 'til 3:00, back to the Duke-mobile and drive like hell across town to school. Start school at four PM. School until eleven

PM. Drive home to MHP. Eat dinner, study. Rinse, lather, and repeat. It wasn't exactly easy, but I got used to it. Saturday nights and Sundays were about the only times I had to play with The Duke, so most of the things I did improvement-wise were small. I did a lot of reading car rags and dreaming on weekends. As the days grew longer and warmer, we started going to Peoria Street, as previously mentioned.

The spring of '79 dawned like a breath of fresh air. We were into a well-oiled routine at school and were clicking off the classes the way your odometer clicks off miles on a long trip; when you're finished, you gape open-mouthed with surprise at the mileage you've racked up and shake your head in wonder. Matt had moved in. He bought the Dart and turned the motor into the Land of Many Small Pieces which found their way into our living room (?!!!) Imagine sitting on your sofa in the living room and turning to set your beer on the end table and finding a 318 block. Once you've taken a couple pulls off your beer, it will stand up just fine in the lifter galley. (Just as long as the fluid level does not exceed the angle of the dangle.) Trust me on this one.

It also works well for holding Doritos and bean dip, as well. Things you didn't know...and probably don't ever care to.

One of the biggest changes to come with the robins of spring was a new job; actually working in the field for which I was training. Somehow or other I managed to get Matt a job with me; this was probably the beginning of the unraveling of our friendship, as he rode to school and work with me in The Duke, and, like a tick on your leg, once you know it's there, it begins to annoy the living hell out of you. Such was Matt; a veritable tick of a guy. I'm a fairly easy-going person by nature. It takes quite a bit of effort to annoy me. Matt put more than a little effort into the task and by the time I left T-town we were barely on speaking terms. Fact of the matter was, I never even said goodbye to the sorry S.O.B. and I'll get to that part later; as it happened. Just suffice it to say he began to annoy the living crap outta me, much more so than Al ever could have. We'll leave it at that for now.

Spring brought other changes as well; for one, it meant the completion of the second phase of school. See, in order to take your first FAA exam, you had to have completed the "General" course with a passing grade, then either "Airframe" or "Powerplant." This would allow you to take the FAA exam for the respective course. In my case, it was "Powerplant." So in the spring of '79 I finished up Powerplant and went down to the local FAA office and took the exam. Results; passing, ninety-eight percent. Shortly thereafter, I received my official FAA certificate in the mail; an Oh-Fishull FAA Aircraft Powerplant license. This was what opened the door for my new job.

This was Big Medicine. Although, in T-Town, licensed mechanics were a dime-a-dozen. T-Town was a veritable A&P mill; flooding the local area with legions of aircraft mechanics of varied (and questionable) skill levels.

It landed me the job, anyway.

With a new job under my belt, and two-thirds of the educational process down, I began to pick up speed and confidence.

Enter "Airframe."

Powerplant had been a piece of cake—a motor is a motor is a motor, be it 340 cube V8 or a 7, 9, 18 or 36 cylinder radial, sporting a pressurized carb and a rotary axial-flow supercharger, or even a turbine engine. Yeah, there were differences, but the Mopar-minded individual could deal with them. Pistons still went up and down, and valves still opened via cam lobes and whatever magic joo-joo went along with it. Turbines was a step off the "norm" path, but the concepts were all the same.

It was "flight controls" and aircraft welding and the like that took a stretch of the Mopar Imagination to grasp.

But I did, and well.

A Tale of Two Dusters
Chapter 15

Learning to Fly

There's something to be said for triumph in the face of adversary. Let's face it; the Powerplant stuff had been a snap for me, compared to some of my classmates. I'd been a motorhead long before this particular chapter of life had come along. I believe scientists will someday identify a motorhead gene on the DNA "spiral staircase" double helix of life. My mom tells stories of me as a little kid following the neighbor, Mr. Olsen, around his back yard with the power mower, making "bbbbbrrrrrr" noises with my lips; see, my Dad had one of those reel-type push mowers. Me; I knew where the action was. Even then the allure of a single-piston Briggs & Stratton thumping up and down had me mesmerized. By the time I was five I was taking shit apart and trying to figure out how to put it back together. I can just see about fifty percent of you readers grinning like a Cheshire cat, 'cause you know exactly what I'm talkin' about, don'cha? Yeah, you do. You've got the gene too. For the rest of you going, "What the bloody hell is he talking about?", just read the story and forget I even mentioned it, OK? (wink, wink)

I took apart my American Flyer train. I took apart anything I could drag home out of the garbage. By the time I was twelve I'd built a bike out of scrap-heap parts and painted it a deep, pleasant forest-green, constructed in secrecy in the cool, damp confines of Dad's basement workshop. Dad's shop was the coolest place on earth (with the exception of Uncle Andy's farm). It was cool, even on the hottest summer days, and had a pleasant, dampish smell; not musty, like a dank dark cave, but rather a pleasant, earthy kind of smell. Dad had this plethora of heavy metal drawers full of nuts, bolts, washers; you name it, it was there. And there was every tool that Ward's Powr-Kraft had ever made, I swear! It was the perfect place to incubate a young, developing motoring-cub and I took full advantage of it. Plus, there was the added advantage that Mom and Dad let me roam free in there, as long as I didn't hurt myself, or break or lose any tools. The rules were pretty cut-and-dry.

Now, back to the bike. I sanded and rattle-canned the rusty old rims a bright, glossy Rustoleum White (mainly because that was the only color available there on the paint shelf in the shop), long before this was considered cool, and shortly thereafter had the coolest (and fastest) Stingray on the block. I felt like a pint-sized James Dean, or Steve McQueen. This bike reeked bad ass!

And then on Bodyman Mike's birthday, his mom and dad took us to see this movie: Evel Knievel.

And so we started in with the jumping.

The jumping began innocently enough; first we built a simple ramp, probably about a foot tall; enough to jump a single garbage can laid on its side. We had a dog-leg back road leading up to this field. The ramp was a straight run off the straight part of the dog-leg, so we could work up a good head of steam on the road leading up to this field, which would then dog-leg right. We would continue straight, over the curb, up the ramp, and jump into the field next to the Bell Telephone maintenance shop. The soft grass of the field would allow us to land and provide cushion in the case of a mishap or botched landing. (Not that we would ever need it.)

Actually, the first couple of attempts went fairly well. Once we had developed a sense of balance and learned to keep the front end up, it became easier and easier to gain altitude and distance. One garbage can graduated to two, and the ramp angle increased as the height grew to two feet, then three. The jumps extended to six feet, then seven, and beyond. And this began to separate the men from the boys (well, the younger boys from the older boys, anyway). The first one to ball it up was Danny P., Mike's younger brother. He caught a handlebar in the gut, bent a wheel, and went home crying. Donny was the next casualty, loosening a tooth and giving himself a black eye in the process. The smaller kids went home, and the table stakes went up.

By this time it was impossible to land on your seat, banana seat or not, sitting down. The correct procedure was to stand up as you launched, lock your down-pedal knee, and flip the rear of the bike sideways, landing on the rear wheel and using your knees as the shock absorbers. Those of us remaining became pretty proficient at doing this and would spend hours practicing in the back field, after the road traffic had died down for the evening. We had a pretty good thing going until Billy came along.

Billy was an older neighborhood kid who was, shall we say, "special." He talked like the cat had his tongue (actually, as if the cat had eaten part of his tongue) and possessed all the intelligence of a dirty wooden tent stake. Being "special," he was treated differently by people and as a result was used to getting his way; in actuality he was a bit of a bully because of it. So when Billy came around and discovered us jumping our ramp, he immediately insisted on giving it a whirl and would not take "no" for an answer when we tried to talk him out of it, insisting that he, too, "Biwwy," would "Dump da Wamp."

Have at it, Billy.

Well, there we were, with our custom Stingray-type 20" bikes and a couple hundred jumps under our belts, and here was Billy the Bully, with nary a jump under his belt on this huge Schwinn touring bike...with a *basket* on the front! Face it; the kid could barely ride a straight line. He rode all the way down to the very end of the street and came barreling towards our rickety little ramp, legs flailing wildly and the bike wobbling back and forth like some bizarre circus act, resembling a praying mantis on steroids. It was much too painful to watch, and far too entertaining not to.

Houston, we have a problem.

The Eagle has landed...on his head.

We were in stitches. We were rolling on the ground in gales of laughter while Billy flailed around like a fish on a dock hooked to a...bicycle? If we'd had a video camera, I'd be living off the royalties yet today—Billy flailing around, blood gushing from his bloody nose and shrieking unintelligible "special" words in that language only a mother could translate. His front wheel was bent over almost double, spokes poking out like a chrome cactus. His handlebars were skewed at an absurd angle, and he was pissed. Wet hornet *pissed*. Billy was pissed at us and pissed at our ramp. And the fact that we were howling and shrieking with laughter didn't help much.

He finally got untangled from the mangled wreckage and began chasing us around in a Benny Hill sort of fashion.

When he couldn't catch us, he turned his fury toward the ramp that had struck the blow of indignity, then onto Mike's garbage cans after making kindling of the ramp. We rode away, leaving him to his destructive ranting, and our ramp-jumping days were over. But we had all learned a little bit about chance, about daring, about pushing the envelope. About free flight, baby. And we kinda liked it.

A Tale of Two Dusters
Chapter 16

Burrs under the Saddle

School was bearing down hard, but we were all getting quite used to it by now. And, with six months to go, there was light at the end of the tunnel. We were able to gauge, pretty well by now, the delicate balance between work, study, and play. The other motorheads and I spent lots of our spare time in the motor boneyards, bargain-shopping, and in the huge discount auto parts warehouse across town. I can't remember the name of it any longer, but we'd kill hours in there dreaming of chrome Christmas ornaments for our own particular tree. Some Saturday nights we'd go down to Peoria street and just breathe in the atmosphere of American Muscle. Other nights we'd take up a collection, fill up the tank of whomever's ship we happened to be crewing that night, and prowl up and down Pine like swashbuckling pirates looking for a stray Z/28 or something of that sort to pounce on. Occasionally, we'd see a couple nice cars at the A&W drive-in and we'd pull in and just shoot the shit for an hour or so—any conversation about any car was a good thing. But truthfully, the majority of our time was spent hitting the books and staring at the light at the end of the tunnel.

One of my newer school buddies was Steve. Steve had a sky-blue, '74 Dart with a 360/auto trans that he just loved to romp on. Steve was a true, dyed-in-the-wool Mopar fanatic. We had many deep conversations over a cold one about Mopar history; the guy was a walking dictionary. He was able to tell me quite a bit about my Dusters, both One and Two, that I never knew. He had the VIN decoders and gave me a little insight as to where my car was built, what year, which options had been installed and the like, and helped confirm the fact that the original engine installed in Hamtramck was not the one I'd bought the car with. He was a good ol' Kansas boy and went back to his hometown after school. We all meant to keep in touch, but then, well...you know the rest.

I found the new job fascinating. I was working for an aircraft crankcase and cylinder repair outfit in Tulsa. My job was to strip, degrease, and ZyGlo inspect the crankcases for cracks (Ultraviolet dye-penetrant inspection) and in a very short time, I got quite good at it. I learned quite a bit about the construction of the engines I would later be working on for a living by doing this as well. I learned where the stress points were, where the cases normally cracked, and this helped me in later years find cracks on engines that normally might have been missed or overlooked. This job would carry me through to the end of school.

Now, I mentioned that I'd managed to get Matt a job with me. He got hired as a cylinder repairman. His job was to grind the cracked areas of the aluminum cylinder heads for the welders to repair. The process was to use a pneumatic grinder with a rotary burr; they would dip the burr in wax to keep the aluminum from clogging up the teeth on the burr. What this also made was one hell of a mess on the floor. Matt would stand in this crap all day, then hop in my car to ride home after work. If I go out in my garage right now, I can pick wax and aluminum chips out of my carpet. I repeatedly asked Matt to clean his shoes before he got in the car, take 'em off, or use the damn floor mat. He chose Option "D"—None of the Above. And so was born the beginning of a huge rift that would have us on non-speaking terms before the end of school...that, and the fact that the guy just plain got on my nerves.

You try to be yourself, and it kinda freaks you out when somebody else tries to be you, too. It got to the point where I couldn't go anywhere or do anything without this guy inviting himself and tagging along. Now, they say imitation is the most sincere form of flattery, but...

Oh, who the hell cares what they say! The guy was irritating; plain and simple. The boys at the Homestead began calling him "Shadow." He never caught on, but I certainly did.

Now, when Matt "drug home" the Dart and took the motor apart and put it in the living room, that was really about the last straw. I couldn't really ask him to move his junk out because, after all, the living room was his "space" and he paid rent. The parts were all degreased and all, and nicely laid out like a dinner table set for the Queen Mother, everything neatly lined up in rows like fine silverware on a napkin. And I had boxes of car stuff in my room...but, the living room? Methinks he went just a wee bit too far. Besides, asking him to move his crap out meant having to speak to him, to communicate, and by now most of our communication was transmitted via grunts and gestures...

Matt: "Working Saturday?"
Me: "Mmmmmph."
Matt: "Can I catch a ride with you?"

Evil eye. Scowl. Squint and a nod.

Matt: "OK, then...I'll ride with you...if you don't mind."

If I don't mind. If I don't mind..."Say, you mind if I borrow your spleen on Monday?"

I'll make sure to jimmy up the passenger door latch and go around a corner real fast, Matt.

Well, OK, it wasn't always that bad. But my patience was wearing thin. Say, did you know that the distributor hole in a Mopar small block is just the right size to lovingly cradle a bottle of beer? I do, and I have Matt to thank for it.

A Tale of Two Dusters
Chapter 17

"Mini"-Me

After Billy and the jumping fiasco, I was once again seduced by the Siren song of the lowly Briggs and Stratton— this time on a mini bike. I always wanted a mini bike, and Dad always wanted me not to have one. Dad always won; go figure. I had the hots for this little Rupp mini bike because it looked like an honest-to-gosh motorcycle (to me, anyway). I sent off for a catalogue and when it arrived a few weeks later, I tore open the manila envelope with trembling hands, and there lay the mother lode—the whole lineup of Rupp ("Live it *Rupp!*" screamed the tag line on the catalogue.) mini bikes in full glossy color; the stuff dreams were made of! I slept with the damn thing under my pillow until it was crumpled and dog-eared. I don't remember exactly which model I fell in love with, but, when I anxiously showed my dad, hoping against all odds that he, too, would be stricken by the agile beauty of this tiny, sensuous, metal-flake minx, he calmly said, "No," and went on to explain why not with a thousand reasons which I never heard because I wasn't listening anymore.

I was crushed. But there is, as we all know, more than one way to skin a cat. If you can't own a mini bike, make friends with someone who can.

I'd had this thing about motorcycles for some time. They made noise. They went without pedaling. They spewed cool, noxious fumes and pissed off old grandma-ladies and various assorted house pets. Evel Knievel rode one. And my cousin David (who was about the coolest dude I'd ever laid eyes on) had one. It was a Honda single, probably a CL-50 or something on that order. He'd let me ride it around the machine shed at Uncle Andy's farm. I was too short to put my feet on the ground, so David took the seat off and let me ride sitting on the bare frame. Around and around. I never wanted to stop! I didn't know how to shift the gears, but who cared?! I was riding a real motorcycle! And that's something you don't just walk away from.

So I made some new friends. It started out with a family who used to live down the block on Prospect but had moved out "to the country;" a farm with land you could roam, and a horse that kicked the living snot out of any kid that came near it. They called the horse "L.D." Hell, we all called the horse L.D....because that's what his name was. It wasn't until a year or so later that out of curiosity I asked why they called the horse L.D. and Kevin, the younger brother, explained that L.D. referred to a description of the measurement of a particular appendage, which we will not discuss here. After that, I always referred to L.D. as "that horse," when I referred to him at all.

But I digress...The major attraction of the farm was that both Kevin and his brother had gotten mini bikes for Christmas. No, not Rupp mini bikes ("Live it *Rupp!*") but mini bikes just the same—Sears brand, I believe. And as long as we could find gas (or "hock it" out of the tractor) we were good to go.

All that summer I spent as much time at their place riding the mini bikes as I could. But like Lisa in the 60s TV sitcom "Green Acres," the farming life was not for them either, so, for whatever reason, they moved back to the house on Prospect, in town.

I'm not going to attempt to recall every mini bike or motorcycle I ever rode; suffice it to say, if the opportunity arose I took it, sometimes carefully orchestrating acts of circumstance with evil ingenuity. I was fascinated by every aspect of motorcycles and motors in general, but mystified by the black magic that went on from within. Bicycles I understood, having built one from nothing but a handful of old parts and a couple cans of spray paint. Motors were a different subject. They oozed mystique and whispered tales of speed and adrenaline rushes. I knew I would own a motorcycle of my own someday, but with the advent of pimples and pitchy voices I suddenly began to start paying attention to girls and cars...

A Tale of Two Dusters
Chapter 18

Hot Rod Heart

...I've got a Hot Rod Heart/Got a one way ticket to the open road, c'mon/Got a redline engine and I'm rarin' to go, put the pedal to the metal, if you wanna ride, if you wanna ride, let's go!

John Fogerty, "Hot Rod Heart"

Two things happened that really piqued my interest. First, two guys moved in across the street with built machines; one a Chevy II with a built 327 and a tunnel ram. This got my attention, like, immediately. The other was a Mach 1 Mustang. I think it was a 351 Cleveland, but I'm sorta foggy on the details. The second, and biggest, eye-opener was my cousin (Well, I'll *call* him that; he was a relative on my dad's side and called Dad "Uncle.") coming to town, unannounced and just showing up on our doorstep, like stray dog. None of us knew him from Adam, but we all took an instant liking to him; he was a likable kind of guy. He had just moved to town to be the manager of a tire store and had found us in the phone book. Our last name was not exactly "Smith" and it didn't take a rocket scientist to make the connection.

Anyway, Steve had this car; it was a '68 or '69 AMX, 390 four-speed, painted pink, of all things, with a huge mural of the Pink Panther on both sides and Pink Panther graphics—all hand-painted by some incredible auto-artist; very professional looking, and to me, very cool. It was also, coincidentally, *bitchin'* fast.

Steve, in addition to being a nice guy, was also a drag-racing fanatic. Being both, he offered to take Dad, me, and my little brother along up to the Lake Geneva drag strip. You didn't need to ask me twice! Here it was that I got my first whiff of nitro-fuel, got to walk with Steve in and around the pit area, and feel the heavy metal thunder of Pro Street motors rattle and buzz my teeth and rock me to the very depths of my soul. I was in absolute awe of these machines, being fourteen and not yet driving. We sat in the stands and watched Steve race; in total awe of this eleven-second AMX we had just driven up here in(!!!), with little more changes than throwing on a pair of slicks and a few tweaks of the Holley perched atop the manifold. I was instantly smitten with the little pink vixen and became an instant muscle car nut and AMC fanatic. Think about this the next time you have the opportunity to reach out to a kid with your own car. Here were two people; Steve and cousin David, who had let me ride the little Honda around the machine shed, who had no idea the profound impact their simple acts of generosity would have on a kid.

We probably went with Steve to the strip three or four times in all, each trip indelibly etching my mind with unforgettable sights and sounds and smells and vibes. After those trips, I would lay awake in bed at night, tossing and turning, replaying the races under the hot summer sun in my mind's eye and hearing once again the rumble of cast iron thunder; smelling the bleach and rubber and hot asphalt of the burnout-box and feeling that excited squirm in my guts as the adrenaline began to flow when the pink missile would launch, clenching my fists and yelling, "Go, Go, *GOOO!*" at the Pink Panther and beaming with pride when he'd win the heat. ("Hey, that's my cousin!") I would restlessly toss and turn under the sheets, unable to sleep, with my senses in full swing as the day would unfold over and over in my head; like a song you just can't ditch, burned deep in your brain's CD drive on a permanent loop.

It was still all magic to me; this motor stuff. I watched intently and listened with my full attention to Steve and the other guys talk—I learned to discern the mild rumble of a street machine from the lumpy, loping idle of a hi-lift roller cam; the crackle and pop of a nitro-fueled rail spitting two-foot blue rooster tails from open headers from the throaty roar of a Z/28 with dual Thrushes; and the asthmatic, wheezing whine of a blown, nitro-fueled motor from the moaning whoooosh of a Rat motor sucking open the secondaries on a Q-Jet. I hungered for the knowledge, the expertise of these guys; to know what made these awe-inspiring Goliaths tick, and what made one tick better than the next. And somewhere, during one of those sleepless, tossing-and-turning nights, I decided that I would have to find out. It called to me, beckoned me—a muscle motor Siren's song.

A trip to the library fixed me up in short order—several books about cars opened some mental doors that had been previously shut tight and securely locked. Slowly, the mechanics of the automobile began to reveal themselves, with the exception of the "black magic" of the motor. This was beyond my grasping the simple contexts. But as summer waned to fall, and a new era began, that of high school, I was bound and determined to crack the code.

———————

There was this "Thing" in high school, called "prerequisite"—translation; you can't take that until you take this. And so it was for auto shop. You had to be a junior and have taken (and passed) Industrial Arts. OK; where do I sign up?

Industrial Arts started off innocently enough with "Drafting." Drafting was interesting, but not very exciting. The next course to come down the road was "Woods." This was more like it. Using sharp, dangerous and potentially deadly power tools was most definitely OK in my book. I learned what a lot of the big stuff in Dad's shop could really do, like routers and table saws, and put it to use, building a gun cabinet and other useful gadgets. Then came "Metals." Suddenly I was getting close to the Holy Grail. I was using lathes, mills, and then gas and arc welding. Next came "Power Mechanics." I had no idea what this was supposed to be...perhaps electricity? (Power?)

———————

The first day of Power Mechanics found us in a small classroom full of...could it be...Briggs and Strattons?!!!!!!!! Row upon row of used and abused thumpers begging to be disassembled! I took notes and listened attentively to the lectures like a C.S.I. on a murder case, while most of the other students napped or spaced out. (You have to understand, spacing out was a frequent occurrence during the Seventies.) It was, like, Week Two, after covering cylinders and pistons, moving on to camshafts and cam timing, that the Big Yellow Light finally came on and the Great Shroud of Mystery was lifted. It was like a miracle healing. Water to wine. Suddenly, I *understood!* What was once black magic, mumbo jumbo, and jibber-jabber requiring a voodoo priestess to translate suddenly clicked and made sense. We were given these pitiful used and abused Briggs motors (which probably should have been euthanized out of pity) to dissect and reassemble like so many biology frogs. The other three guys in my group could care less, frankly; it was interfering in their nap time; so I wrested control of the Briggs away from them and disassembled it by myself in minute detail, then slowly reassembled it like Michelangelo painting the ceiling of the Sistine Chapel. I couldn't wait to hear it run!

A Tale of Two Dusters
Chapter 19

Building Blocks

Fate is fickle. After reassembling the entire motor (practically all by myself) and dreaming of the day I could light it off, the instructor just gaped at me, slack-jawed, when I asked when we got to run the motors. Then he laughed. "Oh, no, no, no; we don't run these things. We can't use gasoline in a school!"

Right. And auto shop was down at the end of the hall, where everyone and their brothers were working on cars chock-full of leaded premium.

I was crestfallen. I'd wanted to hear that thumper pop soooo bad.

And then, as usual, Dad pulled off one of his zingers.

I swear the guy was a freakin' mindreader. Only a few weeks after this disappointment, he comes home from work with not one, but two motors: big, honkin', cast-iron block Wisconsin side-shaft engines, one a seven horse and the other an eight horse. Seems somebody at his job had run the eight horse out of oil, and the seven just wouldn't start or run. He handed me the two motors with a repair/overhaul manual and basically said, "Have fun!"

Boy, did I ever!

I ripped into those things like a monkey on a cupcake. I tore them down to bare nuts and bolts, taking care to make lots of notes, funky diagrams, and cryptic pictures and to keep the parts from the two engines separate from each other. One thing was clearly and painfully obvious; the eight horse motor was junk—scrap iron. As soon as I opened it up I noticed the sharp, pungent odor of scorched motor oil; a smell I've never forgotten. The crank was actually fractured and the rod was welded to the crank journal. It was the first time I'd ever seen blue cylinder walls, looking almost case-hardened with a magical rainbow of different hues. This one was toast, all right. The seven horse turned out to be a horse of a different color. (No pun intended. Well, OK, I did intend it. Sue me.) The flywheel key was sheared, setting the timing off by twenty degrees or more.

As long as I had it apart, I went through every aspect the manual offered: measuring, inspecting, and reassembling by the book; torquing and checking everything as I went. Dad sprung for a new gasket set, and in a few days it was back together...knock on wood. I still remember filling it up with Havoline oil from the garage (Dad was a big Texaco/Havoline fan) and how nauseating that Havoline smelled. Man, that stuff smelled horrible; like dead fish in a garbage can or something! I still won't use it today. I've morphed into a big Castrol fan, myself. Anyway, I hauled this big old (heavy!) motor out to the garage and bolted it to a pallet I had dragged home from behind a factory over by the Bell Telephone facility; site of the now-infamous "Billy-Jumping." I fabricated a pull-rope from a length of clothesline, tied a knot in one end and looped it around a sawed-off hunk of broomstick. I poured about a cup of gas into the tank from the lawn mower gas can (Dad had upgraded to a power mower by this time; the twentieth century had arrived!), wrapped my homemade pull rope around the sheave, crossed my fingers, and pulled. Nothing. Lots of compression, though! Again, and nothing. Hmmm. This was not supposed to be the way things worked. Again, again, and again. Nary a pop. Maybe it needs a bit of choke?

POP, POP, POP! And then it was roaring, full throttle, farting and backfiring. I eased off the choke and it settled into a rhythm: surge, tip in the governor, throttle itself back, then surge again. Over and over! It was running, and I had made it run. Me. I felt like Tom Hanks in *Cast Away* after he created fire. I had dissected the damn frog and brought it back to life! It was a magical moment; to be cherished, dreamed about, remembered.

"SHUT THAT DARN THING OFF!" came the shouts from the house. Oops. I guess I had gotten a bit carried away.

The motor was pinging and ticking as it cooled, the smell of scorched paint and fresh baking Permatex mingled with the nauseating smell of Havoline on my hands and clothes, and the ripe, rich fumes of fuel-laden, burned exhaust that stung my eyes. My ears rang like a five-alarm fire. The Seven Wonders of the World had just unfolded in front of my eyes; if I was a chick, I would've cried. But I wasn't a chick, thank God, so I did what any other motor-mad misfit would do—I fired it up again.

"WILL YOU PLEASE SHUT THAT THING OFF!" Oops. Sorry!

There was no turning back from here, you see. I was in way too deep to be saved at this point and I knew it.

...At the dark end of this bar, what a Beautiful Wreck
you are/When you've gone too far, what a Beautiful
Wreck you are/What a Beautiful, such a Beautiful,
what a Beautiful Wreck youuuu are...

Shawn Mullins, "Beautiful Wreck"

Now, I s'pose, if you're a kid, the coolest thing your pop
can do for you is give you a car to play with. Well, nothing
doing; not in my family, at least. I was still several years away
from getting my license, or Driver's Ed, for that matter.

The next coolest thing he could do is give you a motorcycle.
And when he dragged home this wrecked Honda CL350,
you could'a knocked me over with a feather. Not like in,
"Here's a brand-new, shiny motorcycle for you, Son," Like Pa
Rockefeller might do, but rather, "See what you can do with
this wreck."

And what a beautiful wreck it was. Some guy had T-boned
a car with it. The fork tubes were bent. The frame was bent
and buckled. The front wheel was a pretzel. The lower motor
mount lugs were broken off the cases. But on the bright side,
it was only two years old! Dad had traded a Motorola short-
wave radio for it to the owner of the body shop, Gustafson's,
where it had been towed after the accident, then subsequently
abandoned.

Well, there's no way I could've done it myself. Dad gave
me free rein to take the thing apart, though. Like, *"Here's your*
project, now go to it." I got the motor off; he took it and the
broken lugs to a welding shop, had them TIG welded back on
and re-drilled. Next he found a junk frame. I got to remove
every nut, bolt, and widget from the old frame and transfer
it over to the new frame, starting with the complete wiring
harness. Now, I couldn't have managed any of this without the
oh-fish-ull Honda Shop Manual, painfully translated from
Japanese to English and full of such exuberant euphemisms
as "Upper seat cover don't attached." Dad got a hell of a kick

out of that one; I remember him sitting at the kitchen table laughing until he was red in the face. Anyway, as the winter dragged on into spring and it became much more enjoyable working when you could feel your fingertips, things began to come together. Dad found a couple of used fork tubes to replace the bent ones. He brought the tank and side covers in to the basement workshop and made that his pet project, sanding, priming, and applying a really cool looking green candy-apple metal-flake paint, highlighted by his own hand-pinstripe job. (OK, it was tape; but it looked really good.) He found a serviceable front wheel, and we gave it new shoes; on/off road tires—semi-knobbies. By the first of July that year, it was ready to rock.

I was so excited, I could've peed my pants. I remember we had some trouble getting it to fire, and, when it finally did, it needed some fine tuning; but within a couple of days it was ready for a test hop. I took it out on the front lawn, fired it up, and pulled in the clutch. I snicked 'er down out of neutral and noticed with smug satisfaction that the green neutral light was out. By this time, a cluster of neighborhood kids were crowding around watching the festivities. I rolled on the power and eased out the clutch...

Just about that time, the throttle cable stuck WFO and I did my first wheelie, in front of a crowd, no less! The bike heaved me off like a dog shaking off a flea and lurched to a halt on its side like a mortally wounded buffalo. It embarrassed the hell out of me, but pride notwithstanding, the only damage done was some overturned turf and a bent turn signal. I could feel my cheeks burning like hot branding irons as I slunk back to the garage dragging my wounded Japanese buffalo.

After a brief post-mortem, it was discovered that one of the two throttle cables had been damaged and badly kinked in the T-bone accident. So, Dad went up and bought a new cable assembly and I had it back on in a jiffy. The next day, I tried it again, not feeling near as smug as the day before, and this time it went well. Soon I was cruising up and down the street, until

Dad hollered at me to get it off the road without a license. No problem, Daddy-O! Flushed with success, I asked if I could take it over to The Field. He nodded his OK, followed by, "Be careful!"

The Field was a bunch of vacant land with an abandoned railroad bed running through the middle of it. Once upon a time, the North Shore railroad had traversed these hallowed grounds, before falling victim to the scourge of suburban prosperity where most families actually owned a car. Some even owned two! The land was now vacant and overgrown, although somebody must've owned it, perhaps the railroad still, but we neither knew nor cared. The rails and ties had all been removed years earlier, leaving behind a rail-bed sized swath of pea gravel running down the middle of hills and grassy fields. Now, you weren't supposed to ride motorized vehicles on this path, but this was The Field, and we were in Mudville, and we pretty much did whatever the hell we wanted, so long as nobody's parents hollered at us.

I pushed the bike over to The Field, mindful that Dad was watching to make sure I didn't ride on the street again. When I got there, I fired it up and took off down the trail. I thought I'd died and went to heaven! This was my own bike and I could ride it as much as I wanted! Never mind the fact it was heavy and far from an MX-er; it was a bike and it was mine and I was riding it and just you try and stop me. Yeee-hah! I rode that evening until the sun had slunk below the horizon—a huge, red rubber ball in a sea of violet—and it was too dark to see. I pushed it home hearing the crickets chirping, mosquitos dive-bombing any uncovered inch of flesh, smelling the hot engine smells and raw gasoline and thinking that it didn't get much better than this. And I rode just about every night after that, all summer long. Rain or shine, dry or muddy, I tore up the trails and made new ones of my own, learning to jump the lumbering beast and not do a Billy, fishtailing through mud holes and sending up huge rooster tails of mud in the summer breeze. I beat the hell out of that bike, flogging it relentlessly and taking a few spills in the process, but I kept it clean and well-maintained, changing the oil regularly (yuck... Havoline...*gross!*) and keeping the chain and sprockets lubed and adjusted. That year was the Summer of Honda. My buddy Dave had bought an XL125, Howard had his DR125, and we would ride until it was dark, every single day that we could! None of us wore helmets or protective gear (We considered it "fruity."), which was pretty stupid now that I think about it; but we were just untamed horses running free on open range and no cowpoke was gonna put his lasso around us!

The one thing that did take the wind out of our sails some was the infamous Great Arab Embargo of 1973. Gasoline jumped to fifty cents a gallon! (Gasp!) *If* you could get it. I still remember the cars lined up down the street and around the corner leading up to the Shell station, the signs on the pumps blaring out their shocking news in hastily-scrawled Magic Marker signs: "NO GAS!" *No Shit!* Look at the lines down the street and tell me something I *don't* know. Now, I plead guilty to hocking gas from the mower to curb my Honda jones that summer, but it didn't really hold all that much; a gallon at best. So we rode when we could the rest of the summer until things slowly returned to normal, school began, and the fun was done for the season.

A Tale of Two Dusters
Chapter 20

Of Mice and Men(tals)

...Meanwhile, back at the ranch...

School labored on, and we along with it. The light at the end of the tunnel grew larger, and brighter. It looked as if I was actually gonna make it. By late August I was four classes from finishing. I was talking with some of the guys from school and one of them mentioned "doubling up." I responded by asking him what the hell he was talking about. He explained that, in some cases, students with a B or better GPA were allowed to "double up;" to do one class on the day shift and one on the evening shift! This was terribly intriguing because, if they would allow me to do this for the next two months, I could be home by Christmas! I had enough in my bank account to live on for two months. My sweetie and I had talked often about getting married once I'd finished school. Maybe, if I could pull this off, we wouldn't have to wait until spring.

So I sat down with my counselor and gave him the scoop. He cautioned me that it would be extremely hard, and that if my grades dropped in either class below a B the deal was off; plus, he'd have to get administrative approval. Well, for those of you younger readers who don't feel that grades matter much, here's an example to prove you wrong. I got the green light to start in September, and, so, gave my notice at my job and excitedly called my girl and gave her the news; she was thrilled!

Was it easy? Hell no. But it was a challenge, and I loved challenges.

I dug into this one like I'd dug into the Duster. And I pulled it off. I'd planned my work, then worked my plan. My other classmates thought I was nuts. Why would I want to double the work load, quit my job (loss of income), and rush back home to get married, when I could kick back and skate?

Let's just say I had my reasons; one of which involved trying to get a job before most of the small airports were buried under a foot of Chicago snow and were sending people home instead of hiring. The other one I won't go into.

So early that November, I proudly received my diploma, two months ahead of the rest of my class. My class photo was shot with a bunch of people I barely knew; the guys I'd worked and studied and hung out with for so long still had several months left to go. Including Matt. Now, one Saturday morning just after graduation, I was home packing while Matt was at work. I made myself a bowl of Cheerios and a cup of java and sat down at the kitchen table; a rarity in those times. Usually it was grab a Pop-Tart on the run and wedge it down your craw as you were driving to a) work or b) class (as in the last couple months). There were plenty of Pop-Tart crumbs on the floor of my Duster, and no doubt there was filling and/or frosting on the Hurst T-handle. Anyway, here I was, relishing a rare quiet moment, when the morning sun, which had been lurking behind some morning clouds, popped forth like a jack-in-the-box (Pop Goes the Weasel!) and shone forth in all its radiant glory, streaming in the kitchen window over the sink and warming my back. Fall was a wonderful season in Okie land, and...What the hell...?

A quarter-sized sunbeam danced upon my bowl of Cheerios, like the spotlight in some wee mousie floor show. I stared at it, watching it dance; mystified. I waited in vain for the little mousies to come out dancing with their little canes and hats, but no dice. The sunlight must be reflecting off a mirror outside, or something. You know, how it does that with, say, a wristwatch? Many a cat I've driven to the brink of insanity by simply flicking my wrist back and forth while they madly pursued the sunbeam across the carpeting, vainly trying to kill it with their paws, always mystically just out of reach. I looked around, like that cat, trying to locate the errant sunbeam and its reflective source, but couldn't find it. Then, slowly, I looked up. And as oft-times happens when you gaze at the heavens, things come into focus. But not usually like this...

A quarter-sized hole in the roof let the sun shine in, right above the kitchen table. Perhaps this was why the kitchen light no longer worked, and not a bad bulb as I'd first assumed. This was totally bizarre; how did a hole get there? How long had it been there? And how was this going to affect my security deposit?

Al came home from school in the early afternoon and was as baffled as I was. The mystery didn't get solved until that night when Matt got home from school. When we asked him about our mousie spotlight, his cheeks turned the color of my first Duster, and he spilled the beans. He'd bought himself a shotgun unbeknownst to us, had been cleaning it at the kitchen table, and forgot to remove one of the rifled slugs— the one in the chamber.

Now, I must confess, at this point I seriously pondered which would be the most effective way to remove him from the gene pool; strangulation, blunt trauma to the head, or the simple, effective merciful placement of a steak knife. In the end, I just shook my head and went off to bed mumbling and shaking my head in disbelief, thanking the Lord that the muzzle had been pointing up, rather than left or right, towards either bedroom.

That was the last exchange of words I had with Matt—ever. That episode was the proverbial straw that broke the camel's back. I resumed packing the next day, as Dad was coming down one last time with the Jimmy to haul everything back home. I spent the next couple days unzipping the skirt of the trailer (It was OK to call it a trailer now, because I was leaving.) and hauling out all the Duster parts I'd stashed under there. I hauled 'em off to a boneyard and took what they gave me for them—I think fifteen bucks. I had no time and no leverage to bargain. Everything was packed and ready to go, just waiting for Dad to show. I said my good-byes to Al; despite all our troubles he was really a decent guy at heart and I wished him the best of luck. I never said jack shit to Matt, shit-weasel that he was.

After Dad arrived, we loaded all the stuff we could into the Jimmy and my Duster. We had a late lunch at The Pines restaurant and headed out. I left without saying anything to Broom Hilda and forfeiting my security deposit; I'm sure the damage to the trailer roof and the kitchen wiring was more than the sum of my deposit. I left that for Matt to settle; after all, it was his fault. Deal with it. We got a late afternoon start on the road, heading for St. Louis and Uncle Jim's. The sun was down by 5:00 PM and we drove on in darkness, a tiny wagon train heading for gold country. By late evening I was already in trouble; it had been a very late night, followed by an early morning and I was driving behind Mario Andretti on a two-lane highway threading my way through the inky blackness trying to keep up with two tiny pinpricks of red when the first wave of exhaustion swept over me. The droning rumble of the engine thrumming through my body and soul didn't help matters; the heat was on high defrost and the warm air swirled around my head, making matters worse.

Initially, it was OK; I shook off the first wave and pressed on. But the second wave sorta snuck up on me, and I jerked back to consciousness just as the front wheel touched the gravel on the shoulder. I could just pull over, but Mario would probably not even notice until I was twenty miles behind him. Feeling a twinge of alarm, I hunched forward and dropped the hammer. The Duster leapt forward, eager for a scuffle, and I took a bead on those tiny red dots and just rolled it on. Holy crap! I was pushing ninety and didn't seem to be catching up at all! How fast was he going, anyway? To make matters worse, my eyes were burning, watering, begging me to close them, if only for a second. I shut off the heat and rolled down the window, letting the cold night air blast my face. I popped in *Frampton Comes Alive!* and cranked the volume, hoping to fight off this invisible enemy. *"Do you feel like we do?"* I feel like going to *sleep,* if that's what you feel like, brother! Still, my eyes screamed for sleep. And the cold air was making them water. Every time I blinked, they wanted to stay shut. This wasn't working. Now I was pushing one hundred and finally the dots began to grow a bit larger. I had to roll up the window to shut off the firehose in my eyes. I found them closing once again and I slapped myself on the cheeks and started pinching my leg like some lewd, office pervert to keep from going out again. I felt like I was seconds away from "lights out, game over." Then I got an idea. I began stomping on the bright switch on the floorboard; on, off, on, off, over and over, and finally I saw the brake lights come on like the appearing of angels or something. Mario Andretti slowed and pulled over. I got out and told Dad I was on the verge of being the next Oklahoma traffic fatality, and could he please find a restaurant, truck stop, hot dog stand, anything with coffee—soon! Fortunately, there was one less than ten miles down the road.

Normally, I drink my coffee black, but I was dumping in as much sugar as I could tolerate to get my energy level up. I think I had four steaming mugs of java within twenty minutes; I was so jacked by the time we left I was babbling like the village idiot. I also filled my empty Thermos, just in case. I didn't need it; I was wide awake all the way to East St. Louis, and for quite some time after we got there!

A Tale of Two Dusters
Chapter 21

Rust Never Sleeps

...It's better to burn out; rust never sleeps...

Neil Young

I'd beaten my friend Dave to the punch; he'd been working his tail off at the local Ace Hardware to buy a motorcycle. He came running up to me down the halls of Mudville High all full of piss and vinegar to tell me that he was going to the Honda shop that evening to buy a motorcycle; would I like to come along? Of course, being best buds and all, he wanted me to help him out loading it, etc. But part of it (more than a little) was, of course, to rub my nose in it. See, there was this covert, unspoken competition between us; we were each bound and determined to get a motorcycle before the other one (so we could rub the other's nose in it, natch, and prove ourselves superior to the other). This is rather on the order of one dog marking a tree in another's territory. Now, I'd been busting a gut trying not to tell Dave I had a (slightly bent) motorcycle in the garage already. But I knew that he knew that I didn't have enough saved, and I knew that he knew that he did, and was going to try to trump me by getting a bike first (he'd been talking about it for days), so I'd gone mum the whole week about it, just waiting to blow his Grand Trump...a trump of a trump, if you will. Royal Flush, baby. Spades.

It was spectacular; shooting him down in flames! When he told me about getting his bike, with a vicious, cruel gleam in his eye, I told him sure, I'd go help him. What are buds for? Besides, I needed to order some parts for my bike tonight, anyway.

You'd think I told him he had polio, or a terminal disease or something, the way his face fell. It was spectacular. Of course, he immediately called me a liar and demanded to know what bike I was talking about. He knew I didn't have a bike. How could I remain silent? And so the floodgates burst and I spewed forth excitedly everything I'd been sitting on quietly, and most unbearably, for the last couple of weeks. He promptly reclaimed his place at the top of the heap by reminding me that my bike was not rideable and his was brand new—*Touché*. But I'd gotten my digs in at least, anyway!

So, I went with him. I must admit, my slightly-bent 350 didn't seem quite as cool next to all those shiny, new bikes, especially in the condition it was in at the present time. Dave was buying a brand-new Honda XL125; red tank with new-style vented fuel cap, upswept black pipe, serrated aluminum enduro pegs, trials-type handlebar cross brace, and semi-knobbies on the wheels—quite an upgrade from the ratty SL125s we were used to seeing around The Field. Sure, I was green with envy; who wouldn't be? But I managed to hide it and stay cool, and found a couple Elsinores (remember them?) to drool over; a 125 and the Mother of All MX bikes: the Elsinore 250. Tall, silver, slim; I was in love. Oh well, maybe someday!

So Dave got his Honda, we all got to ride it and that really added the fuel to the fire for my winter bike project, which I've all ready covered in avid detail, which led, of course, to the Glorious Summer of Honda...but then, we covered that.

———

Now when we'd gotten to Uncle Jim's, me being all jacked up on coffee and sugar and all, it was pretty late, but we were ravenous. So Uncle Jim went out and bought a huge box of Church's Fried Chicken, which, at the time, I'd never had before, and we ate until I thought we were gonna puke or pop. Fortunately, we did neither. What we did do (well, at least, speaking for myself) was sleep well. Nothing like a half a box of chicken to switch off the lights; despite the sugar/coffee cocktails I'd had earlier. We all slept in the next morning. No need to rush this time, as it was a one-way trip. Uncle Jim had a big house with a swimming pool and this huge St. Bernard in the back yard, and a dark metallic blue AMC Matador station wagon in the driveway (presumably to haul this monster-dog around in; Jim had no wife or kids). Jim was a high school teacher; theater his forte, and all the kids just loved him, from all accounts. He was hysterically funny, friendly, with an incredible sense of humor and seemed much younger than the mid-forties he was. He loved Santana and The Beatles, which made him extra cool to the younger nieces and nephews. Jim was a rather large man who loved to eat as much as he loved life, and that was a lot. He walked with a very pronounced limp due to a severe accident he'd had in his '67 Corvette (see; told you he was cool!) that had left one leg pretty badly mangled.

Anyway, back to the Matador: the car was a behemoth, rather like the dog it was chosen to haul around—full size, big 304 V8 with factory brushed aluminum mag wheels. For a wagon, it looked pretty cool. It fit Jim's image and demeanor. Anyway, we bid Uncle Jim goodbye after a huge breakfast of pancakes, sausage, bacon, and OJ and motored on our way, having no clue that, in less than a year, Jim would succumb to a massive heart attack in the parking lot outside his favorite restaurant, following a triumphant celebration after a brilliant rendition of a play his theater class had put on at the high school; with his friends, fellow teachers, and students helplessly milling around trying to save him, to no avail. Ahhh, if we only knew some of life's dark mysteries. Little did I know that this was the last time I'd see Jim alive, that I'd come to own that Matador wagon with the mag wheels, and that I would later christen my firstborn Christopher James after this great guy. Maybe it's better that we don't know.

Along with the motorcycles, sophomore year at Mudville High also ushered in new things mechanical; Metal Shop II, in which I learned to use lathes, mills, and do gas and arc welding. After a while, I learned to wear the same old T-shirt under my shirt, so when it came to gas welding, I could doff the regular shirt and have the torch back-flashing merrily away, blowing tiny meteors of molten metal onto the same old perforated, holey T-shirt. (We didn't have such niceties as flashback arrestors back then; you wore goggles and learned to duck.) This way I only ruined one T-shirt at a time, until it was so full of holes it went to the garage for grease rags and I would start on a fresh one. I also took Woods II, where I further learned the mysterious dark secrets and incantations of power tools (Watch that; it'll take your fingers clean off!). I built a gun rack; it turned out fairly nice, if I do say so myself. Sophomore year also introduced me to Howard (that motor-dropping son-of-a-biscuit maker!) who had a Yamaha DT125 and became one of my best friends through my high school years. I still yearned for auto shop, but you had to be a Junior for that, as I mentioned previously, so I continued my self-educational process on my own.

Dad had bought this car: a '68 AMC Javelin with a 290 V8. Now, for those of you who know anything about AMC motors, they are basically all the same; 290 through 401 used the same block, just bigger pie-holes. I knew the 290 was a rather lethargic engine, but I had plans. (This is the way a sixteen-year-old thinks; his dad buys a car and *he* has plans for it! Go figure.). It was pretty cool; metal-flake blue with buckets and a console shift. I envisioned this car (after I would purchase it from my Dad at some ridiculously low price, of course, like...free) with a bored-to-the-max 290, hi-compression pistons, huge roller cam, aluminum hi-rise intake topped off with a big Holley (like a cherry on top!) and a street/strip shift kit in the trans; a true blood-brother to Cousin Steve's pink AMX! I did my homework diligently; I researched all the high-performance info available to me (which at the time, without the use of the not-yet-invented Internet, wasn't much, frankly) and had all the goodies picked out in my mind's eye. This would be a twelve-second car; at least—maybe less!

At least, that is, until my sister Jill, who had just gotten her license, drove it into a farm road ditch and mortally wounded a fence post. We were visiting my aunt downstate and Dad let Jill take it for a spin. The damage wasn't that bad; the hood got bent and the grille cracked, and the radiator and water pump became kissin' cousins; skewered like a cast-iron shish-kabob. Dad got it fixed and runable with a re-cored radiator so we could get it home, but there was still the hood/grille issue. He straightened it out, Bondo'd and primed it, but it kinda spoiled the looks of the car, which, prior to this, had really been pretty cherry.

So, I'd been reading my automotive repair books; learning by the day. Dad had to go overseas on a business trip for a month or so, and Jill seized the opportunity to try to right the wrong. She asked me if I could paint the hood if she paid for materials. I was game; I'd been reading about this kinda stuff. I borrowed a compressor and paint gun from Howard (that motor-droppin' son-of-a-gun). Jill bought all the paint and materials. We pulled the hood, sanded and prepped it, and shot it on some plastic sheeting in the driveway one fine afternoon. I followed the instructions to a "T" and consequently used, I believe, too much air pressure at the gun (45psi) so the paint finish came out a bit rough, but I did OK for my first time painting, and with metal flake at that! I took the grille off and glued the broken plastic with two-part (Holds Two Tons!!!!) epoxy. When it was finished you could barely notice the repairs, even when you knew where to look. When Dad got back, he was surprised to say the least; even a bit moved, I think, that his kids would think to do something like that. I had taken the opportunity to install the optional instrument cluster he'd bought from a boneyard as well; it replaced the speedo/gas gauge with a sport package cluster with speedo/tach and a much smaller gas gauge. It looked pretty tuff, and now it had a tach so I could really wail on it (later, after I learned to drive) and I think he was rather pleased.

———

The trip home gave me plenty of time to think. I figured it was like this; we could wait to get married in the spring, per the original plan, or just jump in, once I'd found a job. In the end, we just jumped. Surprisingly enough, I found a job on the second week I was back. That was the good news. The bad news was, the job was paying less than the factory job I'd left over a year earlier to go to school. It also paid less than the last job I had in Tulsa. But I knew I had to pay my dues, and beggars can't be choosers, so I took it. Right away, I knew this was something I could do for the rest of my career. It had intrigue, romance, and mystique built in. And I happened to be working with several guys who were willing to show me the ropes. I listened, I learned. I also asked a hell of a lot of questions. They say the only stupid question is the one that goes unasked. I won't go that far, as some of the questions I asked were stupid whether I asked them or not, but never mind that.

Long story short: we got married, found a little apartment, and I went to work each day like a real live working stiff. My job was not quite an hour away, maybe fifty minutes if traffic was decent, and driving to work was a real pleasure when you're behind the wheel of The Duke.

There was the usual rush-hour congestion in the towns, but there were stretches of highway that were relatively congestion-free where I could open it up if I felt like it. I felt like it a lot.

My major budding concern was the salt on the roads. The Illinois D.O.T. must have some kind of a deal worked out with the new car dealers—"We'll dump tons upon tons of salt on the roads so that any new car will be utterly destroyed within a ten year period, if you'll give us a kickback for every new car you sell." Rarely does a car last ten years in the Chicago area without showing major rust damage. I was determined to keep my Okie car as rust-free as possible. Okies don't use salt; they believe salt belongs on pork or on the kitchen table. (I concur...people around here oughta learn how to freakin' drive instead of crying for the bad white stuff to go away. People who can't drive in snow shouldn't). Once a week it was down to the car wash. On days when there was snow, slush, or salt on the roads, I tried to drive my wife's car as often as possible. I knew the winters would take a toll on my Duster, so I began to plan ahead. Step One would be to prime and undercoat the car over the summer—like the Red Rocket. Step Two would be to repair the tiny rust areas that were beginning to show around the taillights. As luck would have it, we found a house for rent three miles from the airport at which I worked, which would spare me the salt and highway miles (though I'd miss my morning romps), with a two-car garage, no less! Things were falling into place!

The next unexpected, and unwanted, surprise was Uncle Jim's untimely death. Dad went to the estate sale (Jim was his little brother, after all.) and wound up with a bunch of furniture and stuff and the Matador wagon, which he gave to us. I promptly pulled the Duster into one side of that two car garage and parked it for the duration of the winter and began working on the rust around the taillights...to hell with Step One! The car was running fine; no need to mess with the motor. I'd decided to prep and prime The Duke over the summer and shoot it a candy apple red with white stripes, ever since I'd seen this gorgeous Camaro on Peoria Street one time, it had remained stuck in my memory like a chicken bone lodged in my throat. Over the summer, I began the bodywork in earnest. There were several areas where the paint was bubbling with rust underneath. I attacked these with a vengeance and soon had all the trouble areas taken care of. I had to patch a couple of quarter-sized rust holes around the taillights...Rust never sleeps in the Land of Lincoln...but I'd caught it in time and made short work of it. I spent the early part of summer pulling the front fenders off, priming and undercoating them, and reinstalling them. (Fun with shims and washers!) I also undercoated the problem areas forward of the doors, where salt likes to hitch-hike and hang out. I planned on taking my weeks' vacation and shooting the car in August.

A Tale of Two Dusters
Chapter 22

Pet Sematary

Sophomore year had come and gone; summer was upon us once again. I managed to snag my first "real" job, if you could call it that. My sister Jill's boyfriend, David, worked at a pet cemetery. No, not a *Pet Sematary*, as in the Stephen King novel, where dead things come back to life horribly, well, wrong, like Hanratty's bull or Church the cat, or even worse yet...Gage...this was a real, honest-to-gosh pet cemetery. David's brother, Jack, ran the place. David worked as a grounds keeper and got me a job as an additional grounds keeper, as well as "other things." I wasn't too keen on the idea at first; but, hell, I needed a job if I wanted to support my motorcycle and soon-to-be car habit. It started out OK; I began in the spring just working Saturdays, making vaults. Now, to make vaults, you have this steel form, consisting of an inner and outer form. We would lift the outer form off with a chain hoist (This thing weighed a freakin' ton!), then get a five gallon pail of grease and a brush, and coat the outside of the inner form, and the inside of the outer form with a layer of grease. Then we would lower the outer form back down onto the inner form and secure it. We would shovel in appropriate amounts of sand, gravel, cement, and water into the cement mixer and fire it up. After mixing, we'd shovel the cement into the form, then walk around the perimeter pounding on the sides with rubber mallets to remove all the bubbles. After drying, we'd pop the outer form off with the chain hoist, then lift the cured vault off the inner form and stack it off to the side for further curing. Likewise, there was a form for lids, which we cast the same way. The finished product was two-by-four-by-two feet tall. Once we got a stack of them ready and cured, we painted them with a tar pitch to make them waterproof, then stacked them outside to dry. It was dirty, smelly, hard work. It tore up your hands, your clothes, and your shoes; but it paid fairly well at the time. So what were these cement vaults for? Guess—it was a *pet* cemetery (duh!). That's right, Fido's Final Flea Emporium. State law prevented you from dumping Ol' Roy into a four-foot gopher hole (not that this stopped most people)—there might be an underwater spring nearby or something (There's a comforting thought!). Now, with that in mind, a show of hands please...how many of you have ever buried a pet in the back yard? Mmmm, I thought so. Let me put my hand down and continue typing.

Anyway, once the weather broke, spring had sprung, and things greened up a bit, I was shown how to use the mower. Now, this was more like it; driving a tractor pulling a gang mower! It was machinery (how cool was that?), it made noise, and I was driving (sort of). This was nothing new, as I'd been operating farm machinery at Uncle Andy's farm since I was about thirteen, going up for a month each summer to help bale hay. By the time I was fourteen, I was driving one of the tractors, sometimes the 520, and more often the 3010 (both John Deeres), for days on end. The actual baling took about a week in the field, then another week to get everything stacked in the haymow. Anyway, back to our regularly scheduled program...so driving the tractor/mower at the cemetary was nothing new, but I loved it. Ahhh, the sweet smell of freshly mown grass! I had my transistor radio in my shirt pocket, single earpiece stuck in one ear, sleeveless shirt on, working on a major tan and groovin' to whatever it was we grooved to back in the mid-seventies. Some days I'd lose the shirt altogether. The cool thing was, in June and most of July, the mowing was constant, most every day. Especially when it rained. Things didn't slow down until the dog days of August when the blistering sun nearly scorched the life out of every living thing in sight and the grass quit growing. Then we reluctantly got back to making vaults. I was stashing quite a few bucks in my bank account; not for that Elsinore, as you might think; oh no, I had my sights set on bigger game!

So, I had planned my work, and was set to work my plan. I'd requested an August vacation. The car had been carefully prepped for prime and paint; the paint and primer bought. I'd borrowed Dad's compressor and bought a paint gun. I'd hung the plastic in the garage. This should be child's play for an old pro like myself.

It was all set. The fenders had been primed, undercoated, and reinstalled, then carefully shimmed and aligned with the hood for near picture-perfect alignment; better, in fact than they were before I'd started. I had bought a gallon of sandable primer/sealer premix, for speed and ease of application. All was ready. But as they say, sometimes the best laid plans of mice and men......

It started off great. The primer seemed a bit thick... (strange?) But I imagined that was due to the sandable qualities, and shrugged it off. I started with the roof and worked my way forward, laying a smooth, consistent, yet strangely heavy, coat; across the hood, front left fender, and worked my way down the left side. So far, so good! I'd used probably three-quarters of the gallon by the time I'd shot the right rear quarter. As I filled the cup for the last quart, it seemed, well, thin. There's a reason for that: it was. My mistake; it being a gallon can, I should have poured the whole thing into a large container and evenly mixed it with a paint stirrer. Instead, I'd shaken it upside down, for what I considered to be an adequate period of time. It wasn't. The lighter filler material had risen to the top, or something to that effect. Anyway, what I ended up with was primer that was too thick in the beginning and too thin at the end. The right front fender came out almost see-through. This was tough. I had absolutely no money left and the primer was like $25 a gallon. Crap. Now what?

I'll tell you, now what! Now it was time to discover why you should not have attached garages! My wife, in the house, had been breathing the second-hand fumes for hours now and got very light-headed, dizzy, and almost passed out. Concerned, I dunked the gun in the bucket of cleaner, left it, and drove her to the emergency room. Ever have to wait in an emergency room? By the time we got home, she had a blinding headache (but was OK) and it was late. The next day, with only a couple days of vacation left, I viewed the thin primer disaster and realized that the car would have to be sanded and another gallon shot, this time mixed better! Seems the last quart of thin stuff had burned through the sanded paint on the right front fender and wrinkled it. Plus, I didn't have the money for the primer, and wouldn't have it for a couple weeks, 'til payday.

I can't recall the exact sequence of disastrous events that followed, but they involved overtime at work, miserable, rainy weather followed by a major cold front, unexpected financial difficulties, and the like. What matters, is that the beautiful Carmine Red metal flake enamel never got shot that fall before Old Man Winter moved in. Let's just say that marriage, folks, is quite different than single life, and when you have a wife and a baby and financial obligations, sometimes you tend to overestimate your ability to perform certain tasks within a particular time frame. And all you married-with-kids guys need no further clarification on this, right? Been there, done that? Well, the end result was that the car sat all winter, cold, forlorn, and lonely, with a tarp over it, all the bumpers and trim removed, waiting for the robins of spring...

Now, the money I was saving was for, as I mentioned, bigger game; that being the Javelin. I'd pick it up for a song, then tear into it. Imagine my surprise, then, the day I came home from work and saw this green GMC half-ton pickup in Mom and Dad's driveway. "Now who could be visiting?" I wondered.

Imagine my horror when I found out that it wasn't anyone visiting at all; Dad had bought the Jimmy and used the Javelin as a trade-in. I was, of course, properly horrified. Now what?

Well, I'd had my driver's license for a bit now, had driven the Javelin, and found the handling qualities and acceleration were not quite "all that." So I guess I wasn't too disappointed, after all. By this time, big sister Jill had a car of her own—a '69 SS Nova, deep metalflake blue, these huge L60 rear tires and Cragar mags all around. The car looked like it was going 100 miles an hour sitting in the driveway. Which is where it needed to stay, if it was gonna win any races. This thing was the ultimate pig-in-a-poke. Under the hood lurked; not a 396, not a 327 or even a wimpy l'il 307; but a straight six hooked to a Slip 'n' Slide Powerglide two-speed auto. What an absolute embarrassment of a car! When I'd drive this thing (which was often; Jill let me take it when I couldn't drive the GMC) and dudes would pull up next to me, get a gander at the tires and wheels, and start gunning the motor, I'd slink down in the seat in utter embarrassment, knowing this car couldn't get out of its own way. I don't believe it really ever was an SS Nova. I think the guy that owned it just slapped the SS badges on it. Jill never really liked the car after about the third day of ownership, and a new plan began to formulate, as in; big-block, Rat Motor. Chevy. Nova. Mine. Cheap. I knew you could pick up a used 454 for a couple hundred bucks out of a truck or something. Once I found a 427 Rat Motor in the paper for 600 bucks out of a 'Vette, and drove thirty miles only to find someone had stolen it out from under me an hour earlier with cash on the barrelhead. Rats!

The highlight of Junior year was, of course, Auto Shop. I'd been waiting on this for years. Howard was in the same class, and I think it took the teacher about two weeks to figure out who knew what, and we sorta got the run of the place after that. We were all assigned engines to work on. Howard and I got, not your run-of-the-mill Chevy six or VW engine, but a Ford big block V-8 with a four barrel to work on. Pretty soon we were the darlings of the junior-year auto shop class, helping the other guys get their motors back together and such. When we got into suspension and driveline later that year, it was all new to me and terribly fascinating. Later that year, Howard got his license and his mom gave him the use of one of the family cars; a Chevy Impala with a 350 that needed a valve job, so we yanked the heads and did valves and guides right there in auto shop! It was not unusual for either of us to walk into any class with an armful of books in one hand and a Quadrajet in the other; sliding the Q-jet into the book basket under the desk seat with our books made us feel cool and somewhat dangerous, sorta like James Dean for some reason. I think the chicks dug it as well, although all they did was complain about the stink. Chicks are like that, though. They complain about your dirty, gas-smelling, oil-soaked holey blue jeans, but all the while they're digging it. Anyway, we became known as the "motorheads" or "gearheads" around the school. I didn't mind. Everyone needs something to identify themselves with; for us, this was it.

A Tale of Two Dusters
Chapter 23

Lady in Red

My dreams of building the Javelin had been whisked away like a leaf in a windstorm, and I was still scavenging about for a decent Chevy motor to build for the Nova; preferably, a Rat Motor. Jill was willing to let the car go, for a price, and I had about six hundred bucks in the bank earmarked for this purpose; but not without a decent motor! No way was I gonna drive that lethargic, wheezing pig the way it was, so the search continued. Back in those days, there was no Internet, no eBay, or any of your modern conveniences. If you wanted a motor, it was dig through the want ads, word-of-mouth, or go to the boneyards. The boneyards wanted too much for anything that resembled a performance motor: 454, 427, 396, or 327s. I probably could've picked up a used 350, but I didn't want one. Hell, everybody had a 350. BORING! I didn't like being like everyone else. So I kept searching...

Until that day in October. Senior year. I would spend my study halls in the library, reading. (They would give you a Library Pass for this kinda thing; I guess they figured you'd be studying. Me, I was reading fiction or *Hot Rod* magazine.) So, I walked into the library this fine October day, and there sat Superman. No, not the dude in his underwear and a cape, but this guy we called Superman. (His name sorta sounded somewhat like Superman— someone hung the tag on him and it stuck.) Anyway, there sat Superman at one of the tables, so I sat down and struck up a conversation (quietly). This was a library, man, and "Andy," the librarian, would throw you out if you disturbed him from reading his ever-present newspaper in any way, shape, or form. We even tried to muffle our sneezes.

Superman was the once-neighbor of David (my sister Jill's then-boyfriend). Yes, that's the same pet cemetery David, and that's how I knew him; from David. Superman had shown up at David's house that past summer driving what was, to him, a new car: a 1972 Plymouth Duster, 340, three-speed floor shift, Tor-Red, with black stripes, numbers, and little pissed-off looking tornados on the rear quarters and by the tail lights. I was not much of a Mopar fan at that point in time (still searching for a Rat motor for the Nova); in fact, I knew next to nothing about "brand-X" and didn't care to. I did go for a ride down the street with him though. He turned around in a guy's driveway, then trounced on the gas and left two huge, black stripes shrouded in acrid clouds of rubber-smoke. I remember being fairly impressed. Maybe this Mopar stuff was something to be respected after all...We got back to David's and performed the Sacred-Open-The-

Hood ritual. I remember this huge orange air cleaner with a decal shouting 340 FOUR BARREL! Afterwards, he left, and I don't remember seeing him the rest of the summer...

Until that day in the library. Seems Superman had a little "car trouble" that summer. Accidents. Tickets. Court. Lawyers. And he was looking to get rid of his little red toy to help get him out of trouble. So, he asked me (quietly, so Andy the Librarian wouldn't look up from his paper and blow a gasket) if I knew anybody looking for a car. Cheap. $500 would do. I told him I'd ask around and get back to him.

I think I actually did ask three or four people if they were interested. And then it dawned on me—Duh! Maybe I should check it out for myself.

I ran into Superman in the library again later that week. I arranged to meet him at this truck repair shop, where the tow truck had brought it after his last little, er..."incident."

And so I did.

The car wasn't as bad as I had pictured it in my mind, from the description he'd provided. Yeah, the grille was cracked a little, the front fenders a bit dented on the sides; should pop out fairly easy. The left rear quarter had a huge dent in it; something about rolling on its side in a ditch, and swerving to miss a dog...yeah, OK. Maybe swerving to grab a Red Dog. Anyway, he popped the hood, and there was that big orange cylinder shouting *340 FOUR BARREL!* at me again. It had headers; I hadn't noticed it last summer. He fired it up. Hmmm. Sounded pretty good. I opened the door and crawled in. Comfy. I wrapped my right fist around the shifter knob and worked the linkage. This car had a smell all its own—vinyl, rubber, and gear oil. And something else I couldn't put my finger on. It was somehow...alluring. Low miles, too. Less than 20K and the car was only three years old, give or take a couple months. I peered at the odometer, and then she spoke, softly, almost imperceptibly, "Well, Hello again..."

"Hello *Kitty!* You talkin' to *me?*"

She was. I'd never heard a L'il Red Minx speak before, but when you hear one, well, you know it.

That was pretty much that. She'd taken Superman for a wild ride, and now she had her claws in me and was not about to let go. Meow!

Well, for those of you who've been following this from the beginning, you know how this part ends up. And if you don't, go back and refresh your memory—it's a long, emotional roller-coaster ride. But, as Jim Croce once said in a song, *"... But let's forget all that..."*

...and so, Mr. Peabody said, *"Come along Sherman, we'll leave the '70s behind us for good and use the Wayback Machine to fast forward us to 1981, where we left off."*

And so we arrived in the '80s again—primered car, cold weather, new baby and a new career coupled with a demanding job, with little or nothing left over after payday. I managed to keep The Duke licensed and insured; but with all the window trim off and wearing primer, I didn't drive it. Oh, sure, I'd back it up in the driveway and let the motor warm up to temp, but that was about it. I'd lost the momentum; the wind was down and the sails lay slack against the mast. Oh sure, something would fire me up, and I'd feel that sea breeze stirring, but something always seemed to interfere.

Then I got my new job. It was a job I'd been hoping and praying to get hired on to for months; writing letters, making phone calls, trying to grease the wheels. And that January I succeeded! The new job was about an hour and a half away, so we found a house to rent near my new job and began packing. This meant packing The Duke, as well. Actually, The Duke was one of the last things to go. I shoved all the trim parts in the trunk, gassed it up, and hit the road. I made it without incident, enjoying the thrill of the open road once more. I let the horses run free, as the roads were dry that day. I pulled in the driveway and nestled it into its new two-and-half-car stable and cut the ignition. There was a lot of unpacking to do, and I started my new job on Monday.

Sadly, that was the last time The Duke ever tasted the thrill of the open road. One thing leads to another; money was still very tight, work was demanding, as were family issues. I still had my paint, and I kept thinking and talking about painting this car; getting it back on the road again. But it just never happened. Dave and Jerry had sold their cars long since. Howard still had his Goat, but, sadly, it got rattier and more run down every time I saw it. It was really depressing. The old gang drifted further apart, the wedges of family, debt, work, and obligation driving us further apart every month and the memories of wicked muscle cars and Glory Days fading like the distant memories of summer as you hunker down against the chill of a bitter cold winter. I made a pact with myself, then and there—I would never sell this car. I would let it rot away under a tarp, into tiny orange hills of iron-oxide before I'd ever sell it. Now even Howard was talking about getting rid of the Goat. Not me, I vowed! When we would get together occasionally, invariably the talk would drift, sometimes rather awkwardly, to cars and Glory Days, and someone would ask if I still had the Duster. Still, I would tell them, and always. And their eyes would go glassy; their gaze would go somewhere distant—far off to a time long ago, when they had their early youth and the world by the tail. And again, I would silently vow; not this one. If I let it go, I'll be like those guys; staring off into the distant past, reminiscing and wishing they'd have managed to hold on just a little bit longer, a little tighter. You could see it in their faces, their eyes. You could hear it in their voices. And then the talk would shift, and it would all be swept under the rug, hidden from view, too painful to dwell upon.

The years passed, and I would go out dutifully on the weekends and fire up The Duke, back it out of the garage, and occasionally even spin it around the block; though the license plates had long since expired. But these little jaunts got further and further apart, and pretty soon I was having to charge the battery on Friday night, just so I could get it started on Saturday. And in the winter, it would sit for months at a time, waiting for the first warm spring day to stir my blood. I remember the last day vividly. July, 1986. I fired up The Duke and he swaggered out of the garage, both guns swinging low and daring any cowpoke to draw. I ran it that day until I'm sure the neighbors were quite pissed off. The air cleaner was off, the hood open, and I was checking the timing (just because), goosing the throttle and listening to that hungry dragon snarl, the Holley gulping down huge gulps of air with its characteristic Whoosh! It sounded good; it sounded mean! When I finally pulled it back into the garage, I sat there for just a minute before I switched off the key, taking in the vibes and the thunder and exhaust smell and watching that hood shake the rhumba. Simply wicked! I was, for some reason unknown, strangely reluctant to shut it down that day. It was almost as if it were a premonition, a harbinger of things to come. And when I finally reluctantly thumbed the key off, that soulful, angry little motor gave a shudder and a sigh, and I swear...what sounded eerily like a death rattle.

A Tale of Two Dusters
Chapter 24

The End

This is the end, my only friend, the end...

The Doors

Marion Michael Morrison; aka John Wayne, aka "The Duke," was a Hollywood icon, one of the true immortal stars of the silver screen. The man just oozed toughness. It didn't matter what movie you watched; you knew how it would end. And you didn't care. It just seemed...right! But as tough as John Wayne was on the screen, he was equally tough in real life; a real fighter when it came to life's challenges. But he finally succumbed to the cancer he fought so valiantly. As did another "Duke"...

This was a different cancer; but no less deadly. Chemical name, Iron-oxide, aka "rust."

After that fateful July day, I dutifully charged the battery a few weeks later, with the intent of pissing the neighbors off yet again. But this time it would be different. When I thumbed the key this time, The Duke complained, but wouldn't fire. And then I smelled fuel—lots of it. I jumped out and popped the hood, and much to my dismay saw a river of leaded premium gasoline floating atop the Torker. This time I'd waited too long between runs. The float bowl gaskets had dried up and shrunk, pulling away from the sealing surfaces of the float bowls and leaking like the proverbial sieve. This totally sucked. I knew a rebuild kit for the Holley would go for around fifty bucks (Back then they were only available from performance stores.); and that was about forty-nine more than I had lying around looking for an excuse to be spent. I felt a real need to get The Duke running that day, so I slapped the old AVS onto the Torker using the adapter I'd originally bought for the ThermoQuad and cobbled it together. Dead end. For whatever reasons (probably the fact it had been sitting on the shelf for, oh, seven years or so, untouched) it didn't work either. Well, scratch starting the car that day. I'd have to wait 'til I could kit the Holley. See, back in those days, the parts stores didn't sell individual bowl gaskets. Not around here, anyway.

In the meantime, an event of epic proportions came to be. In front of The Duke sat a steel workbench with a heavy Formica countertop on it that I'd picked up somewhere. The top should have been screwed to the counter, likewise, the counter to the studs on the garage wall. But they weren't. The countertop hung over the edge quite a bit, as well, making it a bit unsteady and front-heavy. And so it came to be, that my son, Chris, was out in the garage "helping me" when he climbed up and sat on the edge of the countertop.

You can probably guess the rest. The whole shebang tipped forward, and whatever had been on top (including Chris) was pitched forward towards the car. Fortunately, Chris was unhurt (though a little shaken up) and the car sustained no damage—except for the rapidly growing green pool of car-plasma beneath it. You guessed it. Something (I don't remember what.) had shish-kabobed the radiator. Run it through. Given it "Green River," as the mountain men would've said. This gave the phrase a totally new meaning, but I failed to see the humor in it at the time. Now I had *two* problems to contend with. I made a few calls; nobody local had any exchanges, and a radiator re-core job was going for around 150 bucks. Great—now I was two hundred smackers in the hole.

It was spring before I got the money up for the carb kit. I went through the entire carb and bagged it. Unfortunately, my luck didn't hold as well with the radiator. Due to the damage incurred along with its age, it just sort of fell apart while moving it one day. The solder holding the seams together just crumbled. Fixing it would no longer be an option.

I'd begun to get worried about the motor sitting for so long. I pulled the plugs a few times, squirted oil down the cylinders, and pulled the engine through. But time finally got ahead of me, and the Duster under the tarp in the garage got fewer and fewer visits. It sorta reminded me of the song "Puff the Magic Dragon;" Puff lost his power as little Jackie Faber grows up and stops playing with (and believing in) him, so Puff slinks off to his cave with his tail between his legs and disappears into the dank, mossy nooks and crannies of his lair, so to speak. That's kinda what happened to The Duke as well.

Out of sight, out of mind they say. A very true statement. Once you lose your mojo, the game is over. Once you stop CPR, the guy on the ground is legally dead. And the same goes for the car under the tarp. I tried to keep it on life support; I really did. I'd go out every so often and pull the plugs, squirt oil into the cylinders, and wrench it through a couple times (the battery was long since dead and buried now). Still, the spectres of rust and decay haunted me, to the point where I finally cracked under the pressure of the fear of the unknown and pulled the rocker covers and intake to have a look-see. Now I could see what I was up against. A little rust on the cam, mostly surface rust, but the valve stems had a thick, scaly growth of rust on them. The cooling system had been open for quite some time now, with the radiator gone, and I envisioned the water jacket all full of hard scale and rust. And I knew if the valve stems were rusty, the cylinders with the open valves couldn't have fared so well either, well-oiled or not. I knew in my heart that, at the very least, the heads needed to come off. This drove the ever-enlarging wedge even further in between the Duke and the open highway. My son, Chris, who as a three-year old used to scream and run into the house when that dragon would snarl and snort, breathing fire in the driveway, now referred to it rather matter-of-factly as "the gwage-cow" (garage-car). Fitting; as that is exactly what it had become. A dinosaur in a museum, to be viewed with respect and a little awe while remembering its former fearsome presence, but just a harmless skeleton of a beast that had once been; held together with wire and bolts but no longer breathing, no fire in its eyes; it could no longer strike terror into the hearts of children, let alone adults. Like John Wayne, The Duke was dead; only to be remembered on celluloid and in the mind's eye of its creator...me.

The difference between the Li'l Red Minx and The Duke was this: the Li'l Red Minx was *physically* gone; removed from my sight, and barely even there in my memory. The Duke was just as "gone" to be sure, but like the mummy of King Tut, there was still a lifeless presence to look at, to remember, to dream about, a sarcophagus full of gold, spices, and untold rare gems all surrounding one very dead guy in an Ace bandage. The garage had become my pyramid in the Valley of the Kings. (The Procol Harum song, "Conquistador," comes to mind.) Over the years, there were numerous fits and starts; I would get fired up at a car show, by a conversation or reading a magazine; go out and spend an hour or so doing something insipid and meaningless. But the reality of the monstrous size and cost of the project held me back. At last, I conceded to logic, deciding I would no longer allow myself to take pieces off that could be lost or damaged until I could launch a full-scale assault on the Duster. I no longer referred to it as The Duke; The Duke was just as stone-dead as the Li'l Red Minx and probably deserved a fitting burial. Over the years I encountered quite a bit of flak over this; old friends would razz me about it—"You still got that hunk of junk?" My wife gave me grief about getting rid of it and freeing up that half of the garage. (Suuuure...when you can pry the keys from my cold, dead hands...) Even my kids ribbed me about it. Chris, now grown up, told me I might as well just give it to him to fix, as it would sit there until I died, at which point he'd get it anyway. (I told him he'd just have a damn long wait, then!) I remembered my vow and dug my heels in...and waited. For what, I wasn't sure. I'd know it when I saw it. This much I knew.

Funny thing was, it didn't happen like that. There was no voice in my head, or a light bulb going on. In fact, it all started with a screw and a motorcycle.

A Tale of Two Dusters
Chapter 25

Awakenings

Question: *Which came first, the chicken or the egg?*
Answer: *Who the hell cares, as long as we get breakfast and dinner out of the deal!*

So, which came first, the motorcycle or the screw?

Actually, it was the motorcycle.

From me, my younger brother, Brian, had also gotten the motorcycle bug at a very young age, but never conquered it. I don't believe he ever *didn't* own a motorcycle from the time he got his driver's license. He started out with a Honda MiniTrail 50 (Remember those?) and ended up owning Dave's Turtle Chaser Honda XL125. He then bought a year-old Yamaha Seca 550 while doing a stint as a motorcycle mechanic for a local dealer. He proceeded to flog this poor steed mercilessly for nearly 40,000 miles and across three states (He made numerous trips from Mudville to Fargo and back, while attending school there!) until 1998, when he decided to get a little newer bike with a little more, ummm, get-up-and-go, shall we say?

He did. He bought a year-old, 1997 Buell M2 Cyclone.

For those of you not acquainted with the M2, it's basically... how can I describe this?...a motor with a seat attached. Scratch that; a BIG motor with a seat attached! Twelve hundred ccs of Harley-Davidson, V-Twin Sportster motor, massaged and tweaked by Buell to pump out 70-something horsepower and 70-something foot-pounds of torque. By my own definition, it's a two-wheeled Hemi 'Cuda.

Naturally, after riding something like that, the Yamaha goes to the back of the garage and begins to collect dust and become a homeless shelter for down-on-their-luck mice. That is, until Big Brother works a deal with Little Brother.

And so it came to be, early in the spring of '99 that I found myself busting knuckles away from work voluntarily. For years, the thought of wrenching out in the garage after wrenching on aircraft all day just didn't trip my trigger. It's like eating too much pizza. I mean, how much pizza can you ram down your craw before you say, "Enough!" It doesn't mean, I found out, that you no longer *like* pizza. You just save some for later! First I did the carbs. Complete strip and clean, with new carb kits. (And you thought Holley parts were expensive!) Homeless mice had been at the air filter, leaving little bits of fuzzy paper mixed with mousie turds, topped off with the pungent aroma of *eau d'mousie*— liquid form, of course. The battery was, of course, junk. So, a couple weeks, a couple hundred bucks, and "Houston, we have ignition!"

Now, if you're wondering why this guy is prattling on about bikes in a car story, I'll come right out and tell ya. It's about the speed, brother! The need for speed! I rediscovered it that summer, not in the heavy thunder of Mopar Muscle, but, rather, in the screeching, banshee wail of four Mikunis stuffing atomized fuel and air through a Gemini four-into-one exhaust with a four-cylinder motor sandwiched like aluminum-flavored Oreo filling in between. Never mind that it wasn't that fast compared to so-called "modern" bikes—it was a fourteen-second missile of fossil-fuel rebirth, and the feelings that I long feared dead and buried burst into flames like a peat bog fire long believed to be extinguished...NOT!

I attacked this new curiosity with relish, and Flitz metal polish. When I brought the bike home, it was rather, shall we say...neglected? Corrosion and dirt covered the wheels and frame. Aluminum surfaces were dull and lusterless. (Little Brother was a *rider,* not a cleaner.) Nothing a good bath and a can of Flitz couldn't handle, though. I remember the first time my brother came over to go riding with me after I'd cleaned it up. I wheeled it out into the sunshine, polished aluminum and paint glinting in the bright sun and said, "Well, whaddya think?" After a long pause, he mumbled, "I think I sold it to ya too cheap." Now, that, folks, is a *compliment!*

We did a lot of rides that summer. A *lot* of rides. And all the time, there was this rumbling in my soul, this whispering in my ear; incomprehensible babble that I couldn't understand or comprehend, but urgent, nonetheless. It was like the gunfighter who, horrified and haunted by his past, changed his name and identity, moved far, far away and became a farmer, swearing to himself to put it all behind him and start a new life. And then one day, by chance, he comes across a gun. Quite by accident, you understand. He picks it up; his fingers unconsciously caress the cold steel, and it feels good; natural in his hand. Like it *belongs* there. And then, as if by magic, it comes to life in his sweaty palms; wheeling and darting back and forth, like a snake, dancing; his thumb unconsciously cocks back the hammer and naturally as a newborn baby drawing a breath, he points it at a tree, or a leaf; the gun barks and thunders and bucks in his palm and the object of its deadly destruction lies blown to bits and mutilated, drilled dead center, without intention, without will, without malice, *without thinking*—naturally. As if meant to be. And his trembling hand recoils and drops the gun in revulsion and horror, unable to fathom the idea that this cold slab of wood and steel becomes a living, breathing thing in his grip—and his alone. It is a part of him that cannot be denied, no matter how hard he tries. Oh, Lord, how he tries!

You could say it was like that. Yeah, you could.

I knew I was in big trouble the first time I whacked that throttle open hard against the stops and heard the wailin' of the banshee trumpeting out through that Gemini four-into-one. Just like that gunfighter-turned-farmer, I knew. I thought I could put it all behind me; forget it with the help of time, live a quiet, sedentary life without the need for speed. Not hardly.

And then came the big turn. It started out as a simple ride. My brother and me—he on his Buell, and me on the Seca, with my fourteen-year-old son, Andrew, on the back. It was innocent enough; a simple, easy country-road ride. My brother was a good riding partner; he led the way but never pushed, never forcing me to overextend my abilities; his were far beyond mine at that point. While I'd "hung up my guns" for the better part of a decade, he had continued to ride and progress in skill. That particular day he'd flagged me on ahead to the lead position. I had no idea where we were going; I just followed the road. Then, out of nowhere, he swung out around me, that Vee-twin thundering out its hemi-reminiscent song, pulled in front of me, signaling a right turn with upswept left arm and gloved hand, leaned the Buell deep into a side road right apex and, with a throaty roar, simply...vanished!

I barely made the turn.

It was if he had been abducted by aliens; gone, vanished, went Bermuda Triangle on me.

I found him waiting patiently at a stop sign, a mile or more down the road, taillight winking a friendly "hello!"

"I WANT ONE OF THOSE!" my mind shrieked.

"I'll see what I can do," said the gunfighter...

The gunfighter was true to his word. Early in '02, I rolled my own M2 off the trailer; a '99 with less than 7,000 miles on it. The '99s boasted 91hp and 89 ft/lbs of torque—all right where you need it; down low. It came with the Buell Thunderstorm heads and pistons (a true hemi-head design) and a lightened crank. There was no wanting for torque on this monster. But the real difference was in the handling; if the Seca was an athlete, then the Buell was an Olympic ballerina on steroids. *Flickable* is the word Buell used. *Unfreakin'-believeable* were the words I used. *Nimble* and *graceful* are some other words that come to mind. Just a nudge on the bar ends and it was leaning peg-deep into the turns; whack on the throttle on the exit and it would stand right back up like one of those Weebles and lunge out of the corners like a tiger springing on a gazelle! This was one scary-fast machine. It sounded mean as well, the Vee-twin giving off a low, guttural growl. At idle, the whole bike would shake, much like a drag car in the pits, rumbling out its baritone, hemi thunder.

True to form, I immediately made a wish-list. My brother's bike was far from stock; he'd upgraded the cams, carb, intake and exhaust, with an oil cooler to boot. He'd also replaced the pistons with Wiseco 10:1s and installed the Thunderstorm heads. This all made for a pretty potent package.

Not to be outdone, I began searching eBay for my own entourage of performance goodies. I ended up finding everything I wanted by patiently waiting, watching, and buying the parts I was looking for. I ended up with all the components used in the Buell race kit including race header and muffler, carbon fiber K&N air filter kit, and race ignition unit—for less than half the retail price. To this I added a Mikuni flat slide HSR-42 carb and Andrews N8 cams. In the fall of '04 I put it up on the lift and, with some trepidation, dug in.

I say with some trepidation because, frankly, the bike was running like a dream. It started and ran well, idled lumpy but evenly (like any good Harley), had great throttle response, and leaked no oil. Well, I had a small rockerbox leak, but nothing serious. But what I was doing was pretty major surgery for a low-mileage, great-running bike. Honestly, I just couldn't help myself. I had to do it. And so, I rolled up my sleeves and dug in.

A Tale of Two Dusters
Chapter 26

Distant Light

I fear we have awakened a sleeping giant and filled him with a terrible resolve...
Admiral Yamamoto, on hearing the news
of the attack on Pearl Harbor

Like the first rays of sunlight venturing bravely forth at the end of the cold, dark night, I began to see something, hear something, feel something. I had that bike spread all over the garage in a heartbeat, going where I didn't think I had the guts to go; deep into the cam case. First off came the airbox, followed by the exhaust, fuel tank, bodywork, then I dove headlong into the engine. Like the guillotine with Marie Antoinette; off with its carb! Rockerbox covers, push rods, ignition box, and pickups; then on to the cam cover, boys! Soon all four cams and lifters lay in my oily palms. I stood back and surveyed the carnage.

Was I clinically *insane?* I had just taken the stuff dreams are made of, financed to the hilt, and scattered the remains all over my garage like a raccoon in a dumpster on Saturday night!

Oh well. No turning back now.

Once I'd leapt this mental hurdle, I found my pace and settled in. I bled down the lifters and began scraping gaskets and cleaning parts. Soon the new N8 cams lay nestled in their spots, timed, clearances checked and re-checked, and slathered in white lithium grease like vanilla frosting on some obscene aluminum birthday cake. New gaskets and seals all around—nothing second best here. Was the cam timing right? I checked and re-checked it; yup, right on. I cautiously reassembled the cam case.

The ignition unit was a snap; a simple Deutsch plug connection and a couple of screws. That was easy. The carb took a little bit of engineering to finagle the enrichener, fuel lines, bowl drain line and VOES switch. Common sense prevailed here. The throttle cable Ty Wraps had to be cut and the cable re-routed to the other side of the frame because the entry angle was different. The air filter kit also took some engineering to get the PCV vent lines set up properly. Finally, the exhaust. The race kit instructions were pretty explicit and all the hardware was actually there. I reassembled the rocker boxes and she lay complete, and ready for the tank and bodywork.

I don't mind telling you I was just a wee bit nervous. If I roached this thing, I would be kicking my own ass for weeks to come. I lowered the lift down to floor level and turned on the fuel petcock. No leaks; a good sign.

I opened the garage door about halfway and grabbed a fire bottle. Drawing a deep breath, I cracked the throttle and immediately smelled gas. Good; accelerator pump working. I switched the key to "ON," gritted my teeth, squinched my eyes, and tapped the starter button—click-thunk-*hmmmmmmm!* I released it. What the...?

Cam timing off? Valve train assembled wrong? Naw, couldn't be. I know my own work better than that.

I tapped it again—click-thunk-*hmmmm*...RAR...RARR... RARRR...

The motor exploded into life, three times as loud as it had been before, and three times as lumpy on the idle. It sounded BITCHIN'!!! The whole garage shook as it filled with thunder and lightning, and I stood there reveling in the sensation. I could smell the new gaskets burning in and the pungent ripe exhaust smell, feel the shaking vibes running through my right hand as it curled around the throttle, and feel the exhaust pulses assaulting my eardrums. I sucked it all in, relishing the victory. And somewhere far off, deep within the bowels of a dark, dank cave, a sleeping dragon's eyes flickered open and he raised his head, shaking off two decades of deep, restless slumber.

Some people take days or even weeks thinking up clever names for their pet machine. It wasn't hard to hang a name on the Li'l Red Minx or The Duke; their personality traits were readily apparent after a short time. In the case of the Buell, however, post-metamorphosis, it strolled right up and introduced itself to *me;* "Hello, Captain, I'm Buellosaurus Rex."

Indeed. Now, "Tyrannosaurus Rex" in Latin translates as "Terrible Lizard." Buellosaurus Rex would translate roughly to "Terrible Buell," or something to that effect. I was not about to dispute his choice of moniker. B. Rex fit; B. Rex it was.

And the similarities between a T. Rex and a B. Rex were soon apparent—on the first post-morph shakedown ride.

Gone were any scattered fragments of good manners and civility that might have been; this was now a hooligan bike bent on frightening small children and animals, and eating them if it could catch them.

There was a slight "dead zone" down low now, between two and three thousand Rpm. It used to pull strong from about 2000 on up, a strong, gradual increase in torque, up to 5000 or so, where it leveled out. Now, the train began pulling at about three thousand, and switched on violently at 4000, pulling like a Clydesdale right up to redline (about 6,800), where I would have a close encounter with the rev-limiter built into the race ignition unit.

WOW!

What a rush!

You could now pounce on this thing off the lights and blow through 90 before hitting fourth gear—with fifth still waiting in the wings—and never hit the throttle stop. In fact, it wasn't until mid-season the following year I actually did put it against the stop. It just wasn't necessary. Besides, it scared the living crap out of me. And all the time there was this unearthly thundering howl in your ears that made the little hairs on the back of my neck stand up. Rolling Thunder, I call it. Whacking the throttle had now become somewhat akin to poking a grizzly bear in the butt with a sharp, pointed stick and nearly as dangerous.

I had to re-learn the lost art of "curbing my enthusiasm." This was like riding an electric-blue powder keg.

Oh, it wasn't all wine and roses. I had a fair amount of jetting to address, but one of the beautiful things about the HSR series Mikuni is that the main jet is accessible without removing the float bowl; but simply by removing the hex drain plug at the bottom of the bowl. A couple of jetting experiments, and I was in the ballpark, anyway.

And what of that poor Seca? Was it doomed to the back of my garage now, until some poor slob rescued it, overthrown by yet another Buell?

Hell no. It became my daily summertime driver; my "work" horse. It's on my lift as I write this, getting new shoes. But, I had other, more serious problems to contend with. A particular dragon had been awakened; a sleeping giant of incredible stature. I knew it, I could sense it, feel it in the thunder and lightning that day in the garage. He had been sleeping for over two decades. Now he was awake—and ravenous.

A Tale of Two Dusters
Chapter 27

To Build a Fire
(With Apologies to Jack London)

...And then one day you find/Ten years have got behind you/No one told you when to run/You missed the starting gun...
Pink Floyd, "Time," *Dark Side of the Moon*

Not to steal any thunder from Jack London, but I'm sure most of you at one time or other during your lifetime have either had to build or tend a fire. You can't build a fire by simply grabbing a log, or several logs, and touching a match to them. Even if you dump lighter fluid on the logs, once the fuel burns off, the flames go out. You need tinder; something to light easily and get the flames burning.

Tinder won't do the job by itself, though. A properly built fire is structured with several large logs at the base, usually in a square, with a small pile of ultra-fine tinder in the center, surrounded by larger tinder (small branches and sticks, etc). Once the tinder is lit and the larger tinder begins burning, you have to sort of hand-feed the fire; keep the tinder coming as it's consumed, until the large logs begin to burn. Soon you'll have a roaring fire, with intense, hot flames leaping into the air and forcing you back away from the heat, perhaps singeing your clothes or hair. But, a roaring fire will quickly burn itself out, exhausting all the fuel as fast as you can heave it on. Not only is this counter-productive to the guy who spent all afternoon gathering or splitting wood, but it can be deadly if you are relying on the heat to sustain you. Far better to let the roaring fire ignite the big logs, then bank it down. The warmth won't be as intense, but the fuel will last a whole lot longer; it will sustain you.

Quite frankly, most of us approach our car hobby like the first fire; we get it burning and then heap so much fuel on it that it becomes a roaring, raging blaze that quickly consumes all the available fuel (time, money, family and job patience) and leaves us, well...cold. In a way, this is what happened with the Li'l Red Minx and the Duke. All the intensity of those years makes you want to rest, let the fire just burn out lazily and slowly smolder out.

Once, while on a camping trip, I kept a campsite fire going nonstop for seven days. At night, when the flames had died down to gently flickering orange embers, I would pile the embers up in a tall pyramid. The next morning, I would spread the pyramid out evenly, throw on some fine tinder, and with a little air, the still-warm embers would ignite the tinder and soon I'd have a blaze going for cooking breakfast. It was much the same with the Duster. For over two decades, the ashes had been piled high under that tarp, cold as a stone on the outside, but maybe still warm at the core? It was time to see if there was enough warmth to ignite a little tinder.

Time had caught up with me, so to speak. You can leave a car under a tarp for two decades. Double that time and the car may still be there, relatively unchanged. But will you be? I was reliving the Glory Days with one of the guys at work, spinning yarns about The Minx and The Duke, and reminiscing. We laughed and joked about it, and I defended my stance on the hulk under the tarp with a bold statement; "Hell, it's been sitting there for twenty-five years, if it sits there another twenty-five, I'll still have it."

He replied, "Yeah, but will you be able to even drive it?"

We laughed it off, but later that evening, the truth of what he'd said began to nag at me.

How long is too long?

Will you even be able to drive it? Nobody knows what the future will bring.

Even if…will you even want to drive it?

Time to find out.

Better to die of exhaustion halfway through the trek than to never start out at all.

I raised the hood and stood there staring. It was not a pretty picture. No carb, no distributor, the old Offy manifold perched on top to cover the lifter galley, Mickey Thompson/Edelbrock rocker covers perched carelessly over the rocker shafts, dirty, corroded, lusterless. I grabbed a trouble light and just started looking, like an undertaker sizing up his next client.

The first thing I noticed was that the left header had a hole rusted through one of the tubes the size of a finishing nail. I grimly noted that I'd be needing new headers yet again. The Pontiac Blue paint was covered with grease and dirt; that is, where it wasn't rusty and peeling off. The water jacket freeze plugs were covered with a white, powdery corrosion. I gingerly lifted off the manifold and looked at the cam. A little surface rust. Some on the lifters and push rods as well. I lifted off the loose rocker covers and was relieved to see the rocker arms and shafts still looked good. But it was still winter, cold and damp. I decided to grab a note pad and begin listing what I wanted to do and what would need replacing. I still had several months to think about this. I put the pieces back and held my hands over the pyramid of ashes. There was warmth in there yet. Yeah, there was.

I fed the small, feeble flame all through the winter, reading *Mopar Muscle* magazine, searching websites, and thumbing through catalogs. I briefly flirted with the idea of doing a full concourse restoration, rebuilding the 340 to stock '72 specs, but soon chucked that idea in the gravel. It just wasn't me. My car had to be, like my Buell, different. Stock just wouldn't do. Relieved to have put that rather disturbing thought behind me, I earnestly began planning the build.

The first thing to do was convince myself that a total teardown of the motor was necessary. It didn't take that much convincing. Low mileage or not, I wanted this thing done right. The next thing was to find a good engine shop. I had no idea whether Sexton Automotive was still in business, and besides, it was over an hour drive, even if it was. No good. My son, Chris, had found a shop in nearby Kenosha, a guy by the name of Tony who seemed pleasant and knowledgeable on the phone, and he invited me up to see his shop.

Not only did I see it, he gave me the grand tour! Not only that, he spent a great deal of time responding to my emails and questions, and seemed to have a genuine knowledge of the smallblock Mopar. I was sold. Relieved to have found a shop I could trust, I pushed forward.

June, 2004.

I had just attended a car show the weekend before. Not much in the way of Mopars, but enticing nonetheless. Spring had come late this year; with winds, rain, and below-normal temperatures that pushed my timetable back some. But the weekend of the car show had been sunny and warm. All systems go.

Now, I mentioned earlier that it started with a motorcycle and a screw. I told you about the motorcycle. Now let me tell you about the screw.

It was a tiny little screw; one that held the fender tag on the left fender well. There were two of them, to be exact. June 27th, 2004. Once again, I raised the hood and stared. I lifted off the manifold and rocker covers once again, but this time I didn't put them back. As I pondered the project ahead, my hand unconsciously picked up a Phillips screwdriver and undid the two tiny Phillips screws holding the fender well tag to the inner fender. I popped the screws and the tag into a Ziplock baggie and labeled it "FW tag", and we were off and running. Just like that.

Four hours later, a heap of similar-looking baggies and assorted parts lay at my feet. The headers, oil filter adapter, alternator hardware, and everything else I could see or reach were loose, including the driveshaft, linkage, cross member bolts, and engine mount bolts. I'd brought the engine hoist home from work in the back of my car; I assembled it, then pushed the car halfway out for some working room. Deep breath; I was ready.

My son and his friend were there to help. Hang time was about fifteen minutes, start to finish, then I set the motor and tranny on my four-wheeled dolly and pushed it out of the way.

An hour later, it was perched on my virgin, never-been-used engine stand and I was tearing into it like a cat on a tunafish sandwich. I knew I had to be careful not to put too much wood on the fire, but the heat felt good. Damn, it felt good!

I didn't have a lot of spare cash to play with—still don't, for that matter. There was a lot I could do without the use of cash early on. There were motor parts to be cleaned, an engine bay to be cleaned and painted, decisions to be made. I succeeded in getting the engine apart, down to the block with just the crank resting like a sleeping baby in its cast-iron crib. I did some cleaning and degreasing of the engine bay and front suspension, trying to decide which way to go with things. At last, a plan emerged through the mist. This car would be redone from the axles up. The front suspension was in poor shape; the rubber bushings dry rotted, brake lines rusty and corroded, tires old and hard. It would hardly make sense to make a twelve-second run at the strip, tromp on the brakes, and have the pedal go to the floor, squirting DOT-3 all over the track and me pissing my pants and doing a Fred Flintstone. That meant pulling the entire front suspension, removing the K-frame, and priming/undercoating every piece of the unibody, and painting or powder coating every single piece of suspension. At this point it dawned on me that it was totally academic whether or not I ever finished the car. It's the journey, not the destination, I tell myself. I also want to avoid the poseur trap so many fall into today. Guy buys a car. Guy sends out the motor, tranny, body and suspension, has the motor built and assembled for him (or worse yet, buys a crate motor), has the whole car assembled, then off for paint and interior, then parades it down Main Street with his chest all puffed out; "Look at me! I have a muscle car! I've spent thousands! I'm important, and Oh, So Fortunate!"

Ummmm...Excuse me...but you're a poseur, nothing but a chucklehead in my book. You did nothing except sign the title and exchange greenbacks for someone else's talent, sweat, and blood. I'm impressed by your machine, but not by you. I'm dazzled by the art, not the artist. That gangly seventeen-year-old in the gray-primer Dart next to you...now, *he's* the one that impresses me. See, he did it all by himself, with the help of his family and friends. No, the Bondo's not perfect and it won't win any awards for concourse restoration, but the kid has a heart the size of New Jersey. Just look at the sweat and blood and emotion he put into this thing!

That's how I see it. Maybe, now, I could afford to have somebody build me a car. Maybe not. No matter, I won't. If I can do it myself, I will. Because I can. So someday, I'll have a hard drive full of digital pix that detail every nut, bolt, every drop of paint, and every drop of blood that goes into building a car like this. I might even paint it myself. (Although I wouldn't feel like Benedict Arnold by having a pro shoot it, this time around. One "Battle of Midway" with kamikazi walrus-flies is enough!) This is not about the car, the finished product. Not at all. It's about the garage-therapy, the struggle, the busted knuckles, and the empty wallet, and the triumphs and victories, however small, that make up a project. And if I never quite finish it, the journey will have been sweet. And I hope you will share it with me.

A Tale of Two Dusters

Epilogue

It's been a grand ride down memory lane, but I guess we've arrived here...in the present time. I'd like to thank you all for riding along. Now don't get all weepy and teary-eyed on me. There's a whole lotta fun left to go and an entire car to build, from the axles up! Part II of this story is gonna go where Part I never had the big brass gonads to; uncharted waters, so to speak. As I promised, this part will be full of pictures, a luxury I didn't have back in the days of Li'l Red Minxes and Dukes. The really cool thing is, I have *no* idea where this will end up, so the surprise will be mine as well as yours. An interesting footnote; this car does not yet have an identity; or shall I say, it has not yet seen fit to introduce itself, as did the Li'l Red Minx,

The Duke, B. Rex, or his li'l sister, the Screaming Banshee. It will happen, though; and as soon as I'm introduced, I'll do the same for all of you. I had a lot of fun burning rubber back in the day, and almost, I think, even more fun telling you all about it. There are memories in this story I've dredged up from who-knows-where that were long forgotten until you all coaxed them to come out and play, and I thank you for that. Now, get in; my motor's getting overheated...and let's go!

A Day in the Country

Summer, 2008

The day started out like any other midsummer Sunday—
relaxed, lazy, a chance to recharge my batteries from the
frenetic work-week schedule I adhere to. I'd overshot my
time window for making the last church service, mainly
due to staying out in my garage workshop the night before,
working on my current restoration project—an '85 Honda
Nighthawk. I had finally got it running after the previous
owner had let it sit for seven years, forlorn and lonely in his
garage, like a lost puppy, while he lavished all his time, money,
and attention on his chrome-spangled Sportster. He'd bought
it as a project from a contractor buddy that had painted his
house and had never ridden it, although he claimed that he

and a buddy had it running. Which I doubt, in retrospect, as one of the first things I did when I got it home was throw it up on the Handy Lift and run a cranking compression check, revealing the lowest "zero" I'd ever seen, which turned out to be both #3 exhaust valves being bent. A lot. And we're not talking thousandths-of-an-inch. We're dealing in fractions here. *Large* fractions. So, I really doubt that it ran, unless, of course, the throttle stuck open and he buried the tach needle in that hinterland far beyond the red zone. Yanking the head, replacing valves and such had me fired up to get this thing popping, and, having achieved success a day or two before, I was impatient and chafing at the bit to get the carbs dialed in—and they were not cooperating. Hence my wee-hours-of-the-morning red-eye party out in the garage.

Which brings us to a bleary-eyed Sunday morning. I poured myself a cup of coffee, made many hours earlier by my wife before she left for work (probably just after I crawled into bed). I took a swallow and my half-closed eyes flung open like a runaway flapping window shade as the "scalded tongue" annunciator light illuminated on my dash. Not only was this stuff the temperature of molten slag on the planet Mercury, it had boiled down to the consistency of hot tar and probably had the strength of concentrated espresso. I mean, I like my coffee strong, but everything has its limits.

After making a kinder, gentler pot of fresh-ground coffee (I buy the beans in the pound-bag. It's *soooo* much better this way) and nuzzling down a bowl of cereal, I stepped out on the deck to have a look around. The past week had been gray and overcast most of the time, with showers threatening most of the days (and making good on the threat, for the most part), with some real eye-poppers during the nights; the kind where you bolt upright in bed, clutching your pillow, eyes popping out like the poor, unfortunate frog who has just been trod upon by a rather heavy-set hiker who has somehow bungled off the trail, all the while thanking your lucky stars that you didn't hang a low-slung chandelier over your pillow.

Today was different. The front that had come through in the middle of the night had brought relief from the heat and near-tropical humidity of the previous week. The air was much drier, and the temperature was down in the seventies. I peered up; not a cloud in the sky, from where I stood. The sky was blue; not like a robin's egg or a serene blue tropical sea, but a brilliant, *electric* blue so intense and bright, your eyes squinted half-closed just gazing upon it.

A beautiful day for a ride, I thought.

This is how I judge things. Not "a beautiful day for a picnic," or "a beautiful day for mowing the lawn," or a "beautiful day to conquer the Western Hemisphere," but always, with the bikes. Everything seems to revolve around the bikes. When I look out and see sheets of rain pouring down in gallons-per-hour, I don't think, "Gee, I wonder if the sump pump is plugged in" or "Maybe I oughta reconsider this whole 'ark thing.'" No, I think, "Man, what a crappy day for riding!" Although, a good friend and coworker of mine, Kenny, the Brit Bike Nut, scoffs at me— he wouldn't let a little thing like a tropical monsoon or a cat five tornado keep *him* from riding. He just shrugs it off; "You have to *dress* for it..."

This was not that kind of a day; this was near-perfect riding weather. Although I had my "marching orders" for the day (aka "Honey-Do list"), it wasn't very big, the wife was at work, and so, who was gonna stop me, anyway?

I pulled on my riding boots, walked out to the garage, and punched the garage door opener button.

Like the door of the Bat Cave, the door wended its way skyward, squeaking, squealing and protesting this gross injustice as garage doors are often wont to do. Paying it no mind, I walked over to my most prized possession—my '99 Buell M2 Cyclone, otherwise known as Buellosaurus Rex; B. Rex for short—and rolled it out into the brilliant-blue, early afternoon light.

Blue Streak blue, full Buell race kit with Andrews N8 cams

and a Mikuni HSR-42 flat slide, all lovingly installed by Yours Truly at great financial sacrifice.

"Whaddya say we go for a spin?"

I got no answer in return, but usually didn't; he was not really the talkative type. I took his taciturn silence as an affirmative on the matter, and mentioned it no more.

I decided to look the bike over before my little jaunt, as was customary. Tires good, gas low, better stop and tank up, oil...well, I normally run the level at the bottom line on the dipstick. The line, and the dipstick were dry. I leveled the bike up and tried again; *still* dry. I peered down the into the oil tank; I could *see* oil down there. "Better top it off anyway," I thought. I walked over to the workbench and was chagrined to find the bottle of H/D 20W50 sitting there only contained about one-quarter quart. I stood the bottle on its wee little head and let it drain into the tank, waiting patiently. Meanwhile, my cat, Dillon, strolled by. He looked at me and meowed expectantly, as if asking to ride along. "In your dreams, cat," I mumbled, as the last few drops of oil dribbled out of the bottle. Acting quite offended at this obvious slight, he raised his tail in an inverted "J," turned his head away, and walked off haughtily with his nose in the air. Now, cats, I've gotta tell ya, they *are* different creatures, all right. If they weren't warm, fuzzy, and flexible, there wouldn't be one left alive. I mean, think about it; they do absolutely *nothing!* They don't come when you call them; or any other time, for that matter; unless they *want* something (food). Then they rub around your calves until you're ready to practice your field goal kicking, as if they're *your very best friend in the whole wide world!* until you feed them; afterwards, they shun you like a leper. They come and go as they please, to hell with your schedule, do what they want *when* they want, expect you to feed them, and don't do a lick of work for it. Dogs, at least they'll try. They'll fetch sticks, or a ball, or bark at small children and mail carriers. And they'll come when you call them. I swear, you could lead a dog to the guillotine simply by snapping your fingers and whistling, and he'll come running, tail wagging and tongue hanging out, and let you lop his head right off. But who wants to pick up a dog? They're heavy, hard and bony, and squirm a lot. Cats, on the other hand, are flexible, warm and fuzzy, and just sort of flow into whatever position you happen to be holding them in (providing they are hungry, and, hence, sociable); sort of like a furry gel. This is what keeps most cats out of the Advanced Burlap Swimming Classes, I'm quite sure.

Also, Dillon is sleek and shiny and black, from head to tail, looking like a character out of *Honey, I Shrunk the Panther* or something. It's as if he is wearing shiny black leathers all the time. He's like the Steve McQueen of cats. He's cool-looking, and he knows it. If cats were motorcycles, Dillon would be a Vincent Black Shadow—most assuredly. (Our previous cat, Domino, on the other hand, would be more like an Ultra Glide, or dare I say it, a Fat Boy.)

But enough about cats...we were going for a ride, were we not? I glanced into the Bat Cave, at my other motorcycle, an '81 Yamaha Seca 550. She sat silently under the cover, shooting dirty looks at us as we prepped for the ride. Her jealousy was apparent, and who could blame her? She hadn't been on the road, or even started this year, grounded at my own hand due to dry-rotted tires and worn out chain and sprockets which I keep meaning to change, but haven't quite gotten around to yet. "Road hog!" she hissed. B. Rex ignored her heckling as I chucked the now-thoroughly empty oil bottle in the trash, put the dipstick back in place, and reinstalled the seat.

"How," you might ask, "do you know B. Rex is a male, and the Seca is a female?"

I dunno. I just do. Motorcycles have their own, distinct personalities, much like people. And like people, once you've figured out your bike's gender, it's easier to figure out your bike, how it will behave and what to expect from it. Think I'm crazy? Well, think about each of your bikes and how it behaves, and how similar traits in a human would stack up. And just see if it doesn't all start making sense. Let me give you some examples. B. Rex is definitely a dude—rough, tough, rugged, and powerfully built. Going for a ride with him is like going for a workout in the gym with a buddy. You're constantly pushing the limits, and pushing each other; sort of an asphalt shoving match. Or arm-wrestling, maybe. One thing I've learned; the Buell is a better motorcycle than I am a rider. His abilities to perform far surpass mine to use that ability.

Now, the Seca; she's a finicky, prissy little *bitch*. There's no other way to describe her. She has stunning, head-turning good looks, fine lines, but can be temperamental and moody; if she doesn't feel like going for a ride, damn it, we're not going. (Unless I call up my workout buddy, Rex, that is.) And she doesn't have the brute strength or low, guttural voice of the Buell either; it's a high-pitched timbre that cuts through your brain like a Ginsu knife when she's howling at you. You can almost feel the dishes flying through the air. She also lacks some of the fine motor skills in the cornering department, but makes up for it by being fun, nimble, and a real scream to ride when she's in the mood. And she gets jealous when I ignore her. You can just *feel* the vibes echoing off the walls of the Bat Cave. But when the throttle is pegged and she's on the pipe, mesmerized by the sound of that four-into-one Gemini wailing up there in No Man's Land, the Red Zone, I get goose bumps all over.

Now, as for the Nighthawk, I haven't owned it long enough to get acquainted with it yet on a first-name basis. I'm sure it'll take a few rides to determine its personality and gender; but trust me, I will.

But I digress (a lot, sometimes). We were going for a ride. I pulled the choke out half way on the Mikuni, turned the fuel petcock to "ON," switched on the key, and bumped the starter. Ever since I put in the big N8 cams, the motor sort of cranks for a moment, then gets lost in the Twilight Zone, sort of like; *ruh-ruhhhhh*...and then a pause. If I release the button for a moment and hit it again, it leaps alive, rumbling and shaking like distant thunder, every nut, bolt, and bit of fiberglass twitching and shaking like it has a severe case of Parkinson's, and then I'll push the choke back in as it lopes and rumbles at a thousand rpm or so until it's warmed up a bit. Meanwhile, I'm busy getting suited up; first come the foam earplugs, which are always such a pain in the ass to get in properly. Either one side or the other never seems to get in properly, sometimes after a ride I'll find one just kind of laying in my ear, like a pillow that won't stay on the bed. Next comes the helmet, with my glasses and sunglasses going on next. Then comes the Vanson Buell jacket and gloves. Today was cool enough that I could zip up the jacket, which is nice, because riding with jacket partially unzipped has a similar effect to holding a black garbage bag out of a car window. The extra drag buffets my head and helmet, making it hard to see and becomes rather annoying. I'd rather sweat it out...but today I wouldn't have to, for once. Punching the button to the Bat Cave, I swung my right leg over the saddle, but before the door touched the concrete, I saw the Seca glaring jealously at us. Was she ever *pissed!*

Not about to let *that* ruin my day, I snicked (on the Buell, it's more like "clunked") it into first, eased out the clutch, and rolled down the driveway into the street.

Stopping for gas about a mile down the road, I topped off Rex with unleaded premium, and reset the trip meter (aka gas gauge) to zero. One hundred and forty miles from topped off to sputtering onto "reserve." Well, 139 miles, to be precise. Maybe less if I get rambunctious. I made a right turn, rolled out onto the beckoning tarmac, and rolled on the power.

As customary, I headed north for the Wisconsin border. Northern Illinois is no place to be riding, with its heavily-populated roads and impatient, stressed-out, multi-tasking drivers. Two lane farm roads are where it's at for me.

The oil thing was gnawing at me; I knew Uke's H-D was open until three on Sundays. I might have enough time to pick up a quart and top off before striking out on an hour-or-more ride. I was paying close attention to the Buell for any symptoms of low oil, monitoring the idiot light and tuning in to the heat rolling off the big Buell motor. Everything seemed in order. I wasn't quite sure what I would do with the extra oil I would have left over; I knew the tank wouldn't hold but maybe a quarter to half a quart; and with no bags, I would either have to carry it with me or throw away the left-overs. I couldn't bear the thought of throwing away half a quart of oil; ultimately, I decided I would stick it in one of my jacket pockets with the neck sticking out like a plastic giraffe. In the end, it didn't matter, because when I reached Uke's, the parking lot was empty and the lights were off. I looked at my cell phone and was surprised to see it was after 3:30 PM. What to do now? Continue to ride, with known low oil level, or head home? Since the bike had been running so well, with no indications of overheating or any other problems, I decided to head out for an hour or so, just ride easy and not flog it as much as usual. I turned right and headed west on highway C at a leisurely clip.

As I crested the first hill, I noticed a gravel driveway with two squad cars parked in it, the officers chatting about something, obviously important, with a long-haired, bearded, big-bellied dude in shorts. Quickly I glanced down and was relieved to see the speedo holding steady at sixty—to my relief. Usually, I'd be cooking along about eighty in this spot. As I continued on down the slope, I leaned back and took in the views and the smells; tall green corn rows on one side, closely cropped hay stubble on the other, the fresh, sweet hay-smell rolling under my visor. Huge rolls of hay lay in the field, a rusty tractor with baler still attached lay as if abandoned near the road. The aroma of fresh manure overpowered the hay-smell, but I didn't mind; in its own, absurd way I enjoyed that, too. The sun beat fiercely, intensely through my visor and the motor thundered out its song between my knees, never missing a beat. Coming onto the curves, I practiced my delayed apexing, waiting until the last minute, then nudging the bars in the opposite direction; counter-steering always gives me a cheap thrill. B. Rex responded in his incredible, usual form, leaning deep into the corners and freaking out the oncoming cars. *Flickable* is the term Buell uses; *Un-Frickin'-Believable* is more precise and to-the-point. Just breathe on this bike and it's in peg-deep with just a feather's touch at the opposite bar-end. Man, I love this motorcycle! Seeing an oncoming incline, I begin to roll on the power; the motor accelerates and handles it with ease. I crest the hill and glance at the speedo—whoops, eighty-five—I ease off, and the motor burbles back as I bleed off speed. It continues to rumble on effortlessly, thundering out its strangely comforting exhaust note that rocks me to my soul. I pass three guys on sportbikes, Tee shirts, shades, doo-rags, and tennies, who fiercely thrust out their left hands in the inverted "Vee" salute (keep the rubber-side down). I return the favor with gloved hand.

Linking up with highway 45, I turn the bike northward and roll it on. Prowling through Bristol, with its 35 mph speed limit, I downshift to third and carry the Rs up high to stay on the cams. The N8s begin to lag if you don't keep on the upside of 2500; 3000 or above is best. I'm soon out of the town limits and crack the throttle again. B. Rex quickly finds 60 again, until I hit the stop lights at Highway 50.

Sitting at the lights, I take time to appreciate the bikes thundering past in front of me on Highway 50. A guy on a Sportster pulls up next to me in the right-turn lane and nods his approval at B. Rex before turning right. As the light changes, I continue northward, banking around the corner and rolling on the power. The Buell surges forward effortlessly as we roll out into the "sticks," I look down and am surprised to see the speedo reading 75. The Buell LOVES to cruise between seventy and eighty; eighty seems to be its comfort zone. The vibes are just perfect, the throttle relaxed; in the zone. Rs just above 3k in fifth gear; this bike could cruise all day at this speed with no effort at all. I head north, for Union

Grove, and whatever lies beyond. The sun beats down on me, radiating comforting, warm sunbeams through my visor, warming me to my soul. The farm smells assail my senses and I can't think of anywhere I'd rather be at the moment. Freedom beckons, and I follow eagerly.

As I ride past the cemetery coming into the outskirts of Union Grove, I think about how good it feels to be alive. Dead people don't ride—best enjoy it while you can.

I throttle back coming into Union Grove, trying to mind the geriatric speed limit. Pulling up to the traffic lights at Highway 11, I make the decision to turn left. The Dairy Queen is a mile or so down the road, and I've had an idea for the last couple of miles or so that a medium vanilla cone might be nice about now. The DQ is a nice haven, a comfortable country ride with a convenient stop right in the middle; a great place to unwind as your bike cools off, while cooling off yourself. You can park your keister at one of the outdoor picnic tables within spitting distance of your bike, smell the freshly mowed grass, and watch the bikes cruise by. And there are a lot of 'em! However, as I drew near the DQ, I decided it was far too nice a day, too *real* to stop, and I cruised past without regret, blipping the throttle in salute.

I followed 11 west as it snaked back out of town, the speed limit creeping back up to 45, then 55. After crossing the railroad tracks, I crossed the intersection of C North, the green road sign informing me that the state correctional center lay several miles down the road. I wanted nothing to do with that; *freedom* was the name of the game today, boys! I continued past, coming to the intersection of 11 and 75. I turned left, back in a southerly direction, (The homeward leg, I thought, with a twinge of regret.) and cruised into Kansasville, which has a population of like, three, and the town's landmark is a biker bar with an old-tyme covered wooden porch, in front of which stood a long line of shiny Harley baggers, probably fifteen or more, and a group of overweight, bearded, beer-bellied bikers milled around the machines in various states of riding garb, if you could call it that. They all looked up as I rumbled slowly past, glaring suspiciously at my funny-looking motorsickle; not sure if they should hate me or not. (It is, after all, a Harley heart beating between my knees.) I rumbled out of that fair burgh and slowly rolled on the throttle as the speed limit relaxed.

Seventy-Five South is a really nice road since they re-paved it. There's a real nice easy, sweeping turn that I love to wind up to and practice my delayed apexing on. Unfortunately, I was behind a mini-van who wasn't into the whole apexing-thing, and sort of spoiled it for me this time. Since we were under the "double-yellow" rules, I backed off and relaxed.

Rather than concentrating on how freakin' slow the mini-van was going, I backed off and viewed the surrounding countryside. There is a stand of pines here, and the Christmassy smell of pine needles wafted into my helmet, flooding me with memories of the piney North Woods, and how I wished I were there right at this moment. The sun warmed me and the breeze cooled me as I drank it all in; you just can't get the same effect in a cage (car). As 75 continues southbound, there's a beautiful stretch of highway lined by stands of pine on either side that goes on unmolested for about five miles or so. The minivan had turned off, and I found myself trailing behind a beat-up contractor's van that had a set of speaker wires with color coded RCA jacks hanging out of the door and bouncing along merrily on the asphalt; red, white and yellow...like jumping, brightly-colored tentacles, I thought. I kept waiting, fascinated, for them to be run over by the left rear tire, but they narrowly kept avoiding death with their frenetic, frantic little death tango. I knew it was just a matter of time before one or more of the merry dancing wires would roll under the tire, and, depending on what the other end was hooked to inside the van, would either tear the wires asunder and fling them airborne toward me; or yank some poor unfortunate piece of video equipment up against the inside door. Or both. The thought of those RCA jacks being set free was a little disconcerting, so the minute the double-yellow changed to dashes, I scanned way up ahead, and, seeing no oncoming traffic, I swung out and rolled it on *hard*.

Up to this point, I'd been taking it easy on B. Rex, sort of loafing along because of the low oil situation. But B. Rex is like a quarter horse in the way that he'll trot along nice and gentle, a well-behaved young yearling; until you loosen the reigns and give him his head. Clenching the bit in his teeth, he shakes his head, leans forward, and digs in; and it's Katie Bar the Door!

We *smoked* past that van with the brightly-colored dancing appendages like it was standing still. I swung back into the right lane and glanced in the rear-view; the van was rapidly disappearing behind me, the way asteroids disappear behind a star-fighter with Doppler-effect intensity. Glancing down, I realized I was clipping along about 90 and relaxed my death-grip on the throttle. I bled off speed back to a more "reasonable" level, as an ear-to-ear grin began to steal over my face. "Damn, you're a wicked one, Rex!" I hollered at the top of my lungs, inside my helmet, to no one in particular. Rex snorted in complete agreement and we continued to thunder on down that thin, black ribbon of yellow-striped asphalt nestled snugly between the towering, fragrant pines.

I was still bleeding off speed when I came to the intersection of 75 and K. Here was where I'd turn left to catch up with 45 South again on my homeward-bound journey. There was a car waiting impatiently at the intersection of K; nose pulled right up to the white line. Rats. I couldn't short-cut the corner. Usually I downshift through fourth and third and make my turns in second. This time, I had to bleed off even more speed; I banked sharply in first, made the turn-a real peg-scraper, then rolled the power back on. The Buell stood right back up as I rolled on the throttle; like a Weeble when you hold its head down, then let go. I couldn't help myself. I gave the Mikuni's slide a healthy dose of tug-o'-war via the twisty-thing in my right hand and let the horses run free—and run, they did. I stayed out of the rev limiter by a hair's breadth, but still managed to thrill myself as I powered up through the gears. There's something about the sound of the Buell motor that differs from other, larger Vee-twins; I've heard it from Sportsters as well. Once it gets above 5 grand, the guttural, rumbling thunder begins to take on a different tone; almost like the snarl of a big cat, like a cougar or a panther, maybe. Twin cams don't get that tone. Nor do any of the water-cooled twins I've heard. It raises the little hairs on the back of my neck!

Once in fifth, I eased off and mellowed out a bit, remembering the oil thing and that I was supposed to be out for a mellow ride today; not "track days."

Now, K is a really nice road with gently inclining hills and long, sweeping turns. It's a road I find a sense of peace on. I arrived back at the 45/K junction feeling rejuvenated, somehow.

I waited on traffic as a string of baggers rumbled by me; perhaps ten or twelve; not a helmet to be seen in the bunch. I shook my head in silent amazement at their self-implied immortality, but realized that, after all, it was their choice. Still, I wouldn't be caught riding without all the gear, all the time (ATGATT). Bike versus cage; bike loses—every time. *Well,* I thought; *not my cross to bear.* And as a pickup and mini-van rolled by and opened up a clearing, Rex and I rolled forward and right and joined in the queue.

Which leads us, eventually back to highway 50 with its four lanes of traffic whizzing by. I decided not to endure the slow-a-thon back through Bristol, and eased over into the left-turn lane. I got the left-turn arrow after a brief couple of seconds and eased Rex into a left turn, but as soon as I hit sixty I had to roll it back off again to turn off onto a slow-'n'-easy country road.

Roads like this give you time to think; time to sort things out. If the world's leaders were given motorcycles and a country road, it would truly be a better place to live.

It's an interesting dance you do; your eyes scan, your unconscious brain processes, and your nerves react; muscles twitch and obey. Yet your conscious mind wrestles with whatever issues loom at the forefront, as if you are on autopilot. You can't be in that place on a busy highway, or when you're flogging the throttle or apexing; but here, on the back roads, leaning back in the saddle, you can solve the world's problems with ideas left over. And for that short time, I did.

But idyllic country roads connect to bigger, faster roads, and soon this one came to an end. Turning left, I got my head back in the game and switched the autopilot off, and once again responded to the Siren's call of power and speed by leaning into the tank a little more and cranking my right wrist back in the comfort zone. Rex took off like a scalded dog, and soon we were doing delayed apexing again and leaning deep into the turns. The Buell is a torque-monster, and with a rev-band between 3000-7800 rpm, you don't have to be high on the pipe or low in gear to get the desired response—it's twist-'n'-go, with torque left over.

Before I knew it, we were rumbling back across the Illinois border, with its stressed-out, hyperactive, and overall rude drivers. I stuck to back roads as much as I could, finally crunching into the gravel of my driveway a full two and a half hours later. Hour ride, huh? Rex seemed none the worse for wear as I opened the door to the Bat Cave. The Seca sat there sulking and pouting, refusing to even glance our way. Meanwhile, Dillon the cat strolled over from the back yard where he had been torturing small rodents, most likely, and purring loudly, began rubbing up against my calves, no doubt brown-nosing for food. I shooed him out of the way and wiped the road grime off Rex on the parts that were cool enough to touch and then jostled him into his spot in the stable.

My neck and shoulder muscles ached from fatigue. Well, I know this sounds weird, but it was a *good* ache. There were still a number of things left to do on the Honey-Do list, and I had wasted more time than I'd realized, so without further ado, I punched the magic button and the door to the Bat Cave squealed shut. Dillon trailed me into the house, complaining about starving to death, so I fed him just to shut his yap. It constantly amazes me that such a small creature can have such a big mouth. Cats are weird, anyway; when they stare up at you, all you see is two big eyes and a nose—no mouth. They should be quiet creatures; but, let one get hungry, and you find out real quick, *Yup! There is a mouth after all! Now, how do I turn this thing off?* Sort of like when you buy a car alarm; such a great idea at first, until it starts blaring at three o'clock in the morning because of thunder or high winds and you want to rip out its little electronic heart, wires still dangling, and pitch it across the yard...But here I said I wasn't going to *talk* about cats any more, and there I go...

I hadn't delved very far into the list by the time the queen got home. She viewed my trying-to-appear-busy self with piercing suspicion. "Didn't get much done, did you?" she queries. "*Not really,*" I mumble, rather matter-of-factly. "So... what *did* you do all day, then?" she asks, still suspicious. "*Nothin' much, really.*"

NOTHING MUCH!!!!? I grabbed a tiger by the tail, poked him in the ass with a sharp stick, jumped on his back and pulled his ears! I rode a wild mustang at full gallop across the open plains, dodging gopher holes and rattlesnakes and shot a buffalo at point-blank range! I cruised the galaxies in a star-fighter with asteroids whizzing inches from my head! I threw a saddle over a Metal-flake blue stick of dynamite and lit the fuse with a match held in my teeth!

Nope, nuthin' much...I'm such a liar!

A Midsummer
Night(hawk)'s Dream

or, "I'm not sure if that hurt,
hit me again!"

With the Duke's motor sitting in limbo, I had just enough time before the weather broke to get myself knee-deep into more trouble. I happened across another motorcycle...cheap... and not running. Did I mention to you that I'm a sucker for bikes? Maybe once or twice? Yeah, I thought so.

Well, among other things, I repair and restore bikes as a sort-of "supplemental income," shall we say? A means to justify an end? Well, this peach looked ripe for the pickin'. The price was right, and, besides, "It runs," said the previous owner, "it just needs the carbs rebuilt...and that's why they're off. I started to rebuild them."

"Then...it doesn't run."

"Oh, no, it runs...I heard it run. From the guy I bought it from."

"And that was...?"

"Seven years ago. It ran for a little bit, then just quit...like it was bad gas or something."

Or Something.

An awkward moment of silence ensued.

"So... it doesn't run."

Clearly, I was exhausting this guy's patience...

"Well, do you want it or not?"

Running or not, the price was right. I had come with cash in hand, prepared to haggle, but it was apparent that road was leading nowhere. Lord knows I did not need this motorcycle, especially since it didn't run, despite what the guy said. It didn't help matters that the tires were low on air and the front brake was locked. (We ended up having to manhandle and drag the thing up on the trailer like a bawling calf on his way to a branding party.) But we'd driven almost an hour to pick it up and I'd paid for my buddy Kenny the Brit Bike Nut's gas and dinner, as well. And it had a clear title. An easy grand or more if it was made to run. My buddy Kenny quipped, "Well, look at it this way. If it's not worth fixing, you can always part it out on eBay and get your money back, plus."

Thanks, pal. I feel *so* much better now.

And so that is how the Nighthawk came to snuggle up next to the Buell and the Seca and The Duke.

* * *

I have this stupid recurring dream that someday, my bike repair biz will finance my car hobby.

The key word here, folks, is *stupid*.

It hasn't yet. Still, I persist.

Forrest Gump's momma said it best. No, not that "box of chocolates" crap, the other pearl of wisdom. "Stupid is as stupid does."

Yeah, that one.

"Or Something" turned out to be yet another one of The Captain's Adventures in Motorsports.

Not only did one of the carbs have a broken-off needle screw, missing pieces, and such; but I decided it would be prudent to run a compression check.

Prudent, my ass. Bad move.

Number one was great—190 psi, nobody could throw stones at that! Life is ducky!

Number two was not as good—150 psi. A forty pound split. Carbon build-up on #1 could account for some of that... maybe. Life is still OK.

Number four was down to 120, more in line with number two. Not stellar, but it should still run with no problems. And this was a cold compression test, after seven years. I could check it again after I'd run it. Life—can't live without it, can't live—oh never mind.

"But wait, Captain," you're saying. "You forgot about number three cylinder."

Oh, did I? Mmmmm, must've forgot to mention it. The fact that number three compression was zero, that is.

Not zero, as in, "Jeez, that's low," but zero as in, "Is this friggin' gauge broken?"

The gauge was not broken.

Off to work, to grab my leakdown tester. We'd get to the bottom of this!

Top Dead Center, #3, with 80 pounds cranked in, and the plot thickens. There was still no pressure. I could hear air flowing though, somewhere; like a little nest of cobras playing hide-and-seek somewhere in the pipes.

How could there be no pressure?

Bring out the soap bubble solution and hose it down. (They don't tell you about this application in the Dawn commercials!) Nary a bubble to be found leaking back through the intake side of #3, which woulda been my first guess. But...I could hear air coming through the intake side of #2, which was totally bizarre and made no sense at all. And I don't mind telling you, it was a little bit on the freaky side! Couldn't be a blown head gasket, because 1-2 were separated from 3-4 with the cam chain tunnel sandwiched in between; two pieces of aluminum rye with a half pound of cam chain salami slathered with 10W40 mustard in between.

I took a pull off my beer and pondered on this anomaly a bit.

I could hear air moving through the exhaust (hence my little nest of peek-a-boo cobras.) Even though the 1-2 exhaust header was separate from 3-4 (it was a four-into-two system), there was a small crossover between the two pipes. Could air be traveling out #3 exhaust port, cross over into the other pipe, back up into #2 exhaust port, into the cylinder and out the still-open intake valves? The #2 piston would have to be at BDC with both sets of valves open, as in the BDC overlap stage—a one-in-a-million shot!

But nothing else made any sense. I decided to drop the exhaust and run the leakdown test again.

With #3 on TDC and 80 psi pumping into the chamber, the gauge still read zero. I peered into the exhaust port with my flashlight and was greeted cheerily by a small hurricane blowing gale force winds in my face.

Quick, think. What else could it be that would *not* require pulling the head?

Maybe the valve was stuck in the guide. Or there was carbon under the valve seat holding the valve open. Staking the valve would show me.

For those of you unaware of the term, *staking the valve* involves putting leakdown pressure in the cylinder at TDC, then using great proficiency and pinpoint precision, wailing on the offending valve with a plastic, rubber, or rawhide mallet with all the subtlety of a Vulcan blacksmith.

I chose plastic that night, if you must know.

So, I went about the task of removing the DOHC setup and its many nasty little slippery henchmen known henceforth as rocker arms. (This is a four-valve-per-cylinder motor with more "henchmen" than Carter's has little pills.)

As soon as the valve train was out of the way, I could see a slight...ummmm...irregularity. Like, one of the two exhaust valves hanging open about a quarter inch.

This was not going according to plan.

(Probably the same thoughts Custer had as the Sioux closed in around him.)

Staking the exhaust valve had no effect whatsoever, unless it made it worse. But how can you tell? It's hard to measure a pressure of less than zero!

It was readily apparent that, like it or not, the head was coming off. And so, with wrenches flying fast and furious, a few minutes later I had opened up the motor like a ripe pineapple.

Flipping the head upside down on the bench, it didn't take a rocket scientist to spot a problem.

The valve was hanging open half an inch! And it was bent.

Now, when I say, "bent," I'm not talking an eensie weensie, two-ten-thousandths of an inch off center, out-of-tolerance.

I'm speaking in eighths of an inch.

Or something. Has a nice ring to it, doesn't it? Could become the next popular catch phrase, no? Like when you get expelled from school. "Uh, mom, I got sent home, or something." Or when you get fired from your job. "Uh, Honey, I got the rest of the week off, or something."

Not that I wasn't expecting something like this. Caveat emptor*, and all that. I knew the odds when I bought it. Still, this "quick-turn" bike might turn into sort of a "lazy-eight" and move The Duke farther toward the back burner.

Still, The Duke was a one-way money pit. Entertainment.

*let the buyer beware

A hobby. And while the 'Hawk fit the latter two categories, it also was a (potential) income source. Spades trump diamonds. And that's why you're reading about motorcycles tonight instead of Mopars.

Well, as I mentioned, the #3 exhaust valve was bent. OK, let me correct that statement; *both* #3 exhaust valves were bent. I found this out after replacing the first one. More on this later. I made a few phone calls and located a source for a new exhaust valve—at $47 per! So I checked eBay and found an entire cylinder head for $35—sounded like a good deal to me! In the long run, it was. Because after I changed the first valve, I decided to check the other one. Logic dictates, if one valve kissed the piston, why wouldn't the other one, as well? Why, indeed? If Archie kissed Veronica, wouldn't it follow that he might kiss Betty, too? (Careful, there Captain, you're dating yourself here with the Archie stuff...) As it turned out, it did. It wasn't readily obvious by looking at it; at least this one closed. But after I pulled the valve and rolled the stem on a flat surface, the wobble—and the ugly truth—were pretty evident. Hey, no problem! I had an extra head chock full of free $47 exhaust valves! (big grin!)

It was a short night's work to pull the valves, clean them up, and lap the seats. I slapped them in and went about reassembling the whole mess. As it turned out, I ended up finding several collapsed lifters. Just happened to have extra ones with my eBay head! so that didn't set me back at all. Not one bit! So after a bit of work, the whole shebang was back together and looking as unmolested as when I'd started. So, now for the moment of truth, I ran a cranking compression test and wound up with 180 psi—even better than I'd hoped for!

Now what to do about carbs? The missing parts from the carb bank were (as usual) way more expensive than a whole bank of rebuilt carbs which, incidentally, was way more than I wanted to spend to begin with. Fortunately, I found a complete set of carbs on eBay for a reasonable price and snatched them up. The intention was to cannibalize parts off these and use them on my original carbs, but they were clean enough and the bank was complete, so after pulling the bowls and slides, blasting them with a little GumOut and compressed air, and checking the jets, I just used them as-is instead.

Now, usually, a motor that has not run in seven years will give you a run for your money trying to achieve lift-off. Not this one! I don't think the crank made even one complete revolution before it roared to life, causing yet another big grin to appear on my mug! "Who's yer daddy?!!!" I howled gleefully to a rather annoyed-looking Buellosaurus Rex, who couldn't care less about any Jap motorcycles, and this one in particular. The Duke stirred, but stayed soundly asleep.

Oh, sure, I've still got some issues to deal with, but the biggest hurdle has been leapt. "NOW it runs, Mister!" I mumbled under my breath, to no one in particular, as if the previous owner could actually hear me. There are times, I'll admit, especially when I'm "in the groove," that if I were somebody else, I'd likely find myself rather obnoxious. Most of you motorheads know exactly what I mean. We tend to get rather cocky about our mechanical prowess at times, and this was one of them. I didn't revel in my mechanical mastery too very long, though, for I noticed a pool of gas collecting on the motor—one of the carb joints was leaking, most likely a dried-up seal. So the carbs would have to come off yet again, for the third time. (First time was for a leaking fuel inlet Tee, the second time for a choke issue.) But hey, it runs. For real, this time. I know The Duke would approve!

So off they came. It was, as I suspected, a dried up joint seal. No problem. I had extra parts, remember? Back on they went, this time with no leaks. A quick tweak with the long #2 Phillips and the mercury gauges (carb sticks), and they were all reasonably synched—lickety split. Meanwhile, eBay parts were arriving daily. First the new tail light, then the new front signals. Before long, this thing might be ready for a merciless test flogging!

Once the re-assembly was complete, it was time to go after the tuning. The bike started and ran well on the lift. But how would it ride?

I'd managed to snag a pristine seat off eBay, looking like NOS (New Old Stock) and a perfect fit. I'd been borrowing the battery from the Seca, and though it fit inside the battery box, it was not a good fit in the true sense of the word. Besides, the Seca was giving me the evil-eye every time I walked past. Sigh. Off to Auto Zone and whip out the checkbook. Again.

I also have to mention, at this point, that I'd been running off my remote tank hanging above the lift. The 'Hawk tank was pretty rusty inside, with lots of indescribable goo as well. I decided to flush it.

No, not down the toilet! Flush it out, as in acid dip.

First, off to Ace Hardware for a quart of muriatic acid. Then, remove the fuel cap, petcock, and fuel quantity transmitter and plug up the holes.

I used plastic CaPlugs for the openings and sealed them with aluminum tape (except for the fuel filler opening; that was left open to pour in the muriatic acid).

WARNING: Should you attempt to maneuver this

maneuver, wear eye protection, rubber gloves, and clothing that you don't want to keep any longer!

I performed this ancient tribal ritual in a plastic deep-sink with running HOT water, and a hose with hot water and a spray nozzle available as well.

Here's the rundown.

Goggles on, gloves on, pour in about a cup of muriatic acid (straight up) and...quickly...tape off the opening with layers of aluminum tape as gases begin to spew forth like Vesuvius gassing at Pompeii. Gently rocking and tipping the tank, I can hear the fizzing and bubbling, as the taped-off opening begins to bulge. A whole lotta gassin' goin' on in there, my brotha! I set my watch for ten minutes, unsure if I was gonna burn a hole through the aluminum tape, or worse yet, right through the tank. I figured (correctly so) that the tape would give out before the tank.

I continued to rock, tip, and agitate the tank. As luck would have it, neither tank nor tape gave out. After the designated allotted time, I removed the amazing magical tape, and, turning my head to avoid the blast of noxious fumes rising like heat waves shimmering off a hot blacktop highway in August, poured the contents into the sink.

EeeeGADS!!!!!

Where did all that crap come from!!!!!?????

The bottom of the deep sink looked like the hull of the Titanic resting peacefully at the bottom of the Atlantic! I turned on the hot water and began filling the tank, alternating rinsing and dumping, until I felt it was reasonably neutralized. With a flashlight and mirror I peered inside to survey the wreckage.

What I saw was both encouraging and discouraging, in a word.

First of all, I realized I wasn't finished. Large scaly areas of rust still existed, like moss on a boulder. Yet, where the acid had been allowed to work unencumbered, the metal shone through like a new penny—bright and sparkly-clean!

Since the tape and tank showed no adverse effects, I decided to double the recipe; twice the acid for twice the time.

To make a long story short(er), I ended up doing the tank three times over, and using up the entire quart of acid. But when I was finished, it shone as if brand-new. Since I knew it would be a few days before I fueled it up, surface (flash) rust was a concern, so I sloshed the tank with LPS II (a light oil) and left it plugged. The spray nozzle had knocked a lot of rust loose during the repeated rinsings, and, all in all, I probably washed half a cup of rust flakes down the drain. And people wonder why they keep clogging their pilot jets, season after season.

Armed with a reasonably clean tank, I flushed the LPS out, cleaned and reinstalled the petcock, fuel transmitter, and fuel cap. The paint was totally unaffected by the acid, and I'd been cautious to keep it away from the decals. I replaced the fuel line, installed a ninety-degree filter, and installed the airbox boots and "phony velocity stacks" (not sure what Honda calls these) I'd snagged off eBay. I'd wrestled with trying to find a set of rear turn signals; the signals themselves looked fine, but the flexible stalks were broken. None of the used signals had stalks (Wonder why?) and new parts were almost $75, which I couldn't bear to part with for big old fugly-looking "Prince Charles" signals. In the end, I found a nice set of sleek little Lockhart-Phillips signals that looked like they simply belonged there; and they wouldn't smack the cars in the oncoming traffic lane if I wandered a bit too close to the double-yellow.

In went the new battery. I discovered the battery box bracket that should have been there wasn't, nor were the bolts to hold it in place, which was, most likely, the reason the bracket wasn't there...duh!

So, call up the folks at Bike Bandit (who I was getting to know on a first-name basis!) and order some more parts. Finally, I felt I was ready.

You'd think what with all the commotion last Sunday, with B. Rex going out for the maiden voyage of 2010 and all (albeit short and chilly) that Lazzy would have awakened. But no, he lay curled up in hibernation, much like a sleeping bear. I pulled the cover off and even motored him over, but he wasn't biting. "Leave me alone," he seemed to mumble sleepily. Since the day was getting late, I let it ride.

Not so, today. Though there lay a fresh three inches of snow around from Saturday's freak storm, it was warming up, and, after returning from several hours of working on the Interceptor, I was determined to push the issue. Knowing from last weekend that the battery was somewhat lethargic, I pulled the retainer and hooked up the trickle charger. Since I'd already committed the mortal sin last week of turning on the fuel and filling the float bowls, it was do-or-die. I wheeled Rex out of the way, and just for the hell of it, fired it up and let it idle. Since I got nary a pop out of Lazzy last week, I decided to circumvent normal operating procedure, and popped the air filter out and gave Lazzy a quick blast of starting fluid. Since it had been charging for a few, I slid the battery back in, gave it full choke, and crossed my fingers.

Like a man awakened from R.E.M. sleep by a home intruder, Lazzy let out a surprised yelp and barked to life, thumping evenly on all four! While he rumbled at high-idle, I quickly replaced the filter and cover, battery box holder, and side cover and seat, then eased off the choke until he purred nicely. I let him run a good ten or fifteen minutes, until the garage was filed with fumes despite the open door, then switched off the key.

"Good Morning, Sunshine!" I quipped. "Welcome back!" If bikes could smile, I think I saw one.

Hey, it wasn't me. Honest! I was irritated, but had it under control. See, I was heading home after a relaxing ride tonight, Lazzy doing well, save for the spongy, slightly wonky front forks, that have since ceased to leak fluid (quite likely because they're friggin' empty, common sense whispers); anyway... Lazzy running well and nicely behaved until some putz in an SUV pulls out in front—I mean, RIGHT in front—of us, and then proceeds to lumber down the road like a B-17 on a takeoff roll. Damn you! There was nobody behind us; I had checked the mirrors. No reason why you couldn't have waited another 10 seconds, and I snarl and let loose a stream of oaths inside my helmet as I'm starting to haul down on the binders. Then Lazzy surprises us both by, without warning, deftly flicking left, activating the signal, and subsequently pinning the throttle against the stop as the motor magically blips down into fifth and begins to howl like a hyena at full chat, streaking by said moron like a red-on-black comet, then tucking neatly back into his own lane to avoid the oncoming traffic.

"You little shit!" I scold him, chastising, while at the same time grinning from ear to ear—but he can't see that, of course, from outside the helmet.

"Next time, at least give me some warning!"

Stoic silence from Lazarus, save for the wind rushing past my ears and the howl of the exhaust.

As I push him back in the garage, still scowling and murmuring under my breath, I take a little extra care wiping him down. He cuts a very handsome profile in the setting sunlight. One very wicked looking motorsickle, I muse.

I've gotta watch this one, I tell myself. There's still some unbroken spirit left here in this old hoss.

Captain Tells Lazzy
"Get Lost!"

Oh, hell, no! Not THAT way! And you thought I was giving Lazzie the boot?

No, nothing like that. What it was, was like this......

It's been a few weeks, I s'pose. The last couple of weekends have just seemed right for riding Buellosaurus, I guess; and so Lazzie has been sitting with his weeping fork seal, rather forlornly in the garage.

Friday, I rode him to work...just because. Work is only a mile or so. Lazzy started right up, but took a while to warm up, and was sluggish off-idle. Hmmmmm. Sounds like he needs a good thrashing; leaking fork seal or not.

So today, I let the thrashing begin. Topped him off with gas and headed out in the usual direction. Lazzie was a bit finicky for the first mile or two, but after a couple runs through the gears, began to settle in.

Now, I don't know if the rest of you do; but I have a "usual circuit," with variances, of course, that I ride that's about 65 miles or so. Nice, open highway and farm country. By the time I return, my neck and shoulders usually hurt, my back is stiff, and my ears are ringing like Sunday church bells if I'm on the Buellosaurus, sometimes even with ear plugs. So, I'm usually quite ready to roll the offending vehicle into the garage and go about my business, having scratched that particular itch.

Today was different.

The last few rides, I've found myself passing roads I've passed a hundred times before, and wondering just where the heck they went. I was doing the same thing today; wondering, aloud; when Lazzie jumped into the conversation, unsolicited.

(Me) *I wonder where that road goes?*

(Lazzie) West, by the looks of it.

Smartass.

Well, if I was driving, I'd go find out!

Oh, would you now? OK, then; you're driving.

A sort of mental "tossing of the keys" took place then, and I was just along for the ride in uncharted waters.

The first thing Lazzie does is hang a left at an intersection I've driven through at least a hundred times. Hmmm. This is a pretty cool road. Wonder why I've never gone down this way? We head west, me wondering if and when Lazarus is gonna alter course. He does, and now we are northbound. More small towns, more new scenery, more serene country highways I've never traveled. Plenty of gas, plenty of daylight, plenty of time. No hurry to get home today; the wifey's at work and there's no place I have to be for the next couple of hours. Lead on, Lazzie!

I recognize places; places I've ridden through before with my brother, highways I cross that I've traveled on, always crossing the one I'm riding. Small, quiet southern Wisconsin towns, names I recognize.

"Are you lost?" I query

"Yes...and no," comes the answer. "I have a basic sense of

direction where I'm going. No need to dig out a map. I'll get us back OK."

I shrug. "*You're* driving."

All the while, Lazzie purrs like a kitten that just found an open carton of milk. Nary a hiccup. The front fork feels a bit spongy is all, but nothing drastic. We press on.

Finally we're in semi-familiar territory. Lazzie banks southeast and we lazily wend our way back, taking every out-of-the-way off road we can find, until we can no longer find roads we don't know. The sun shines brightly, warming me through the leathers, but the air is cool and just about as perfect as you could wish for.

Finally, we arrive home. How long have we been gone? Several hours, at least. I put Lazzie away and turn on the garage fan to cool the toasty-warm motor. I wipe some of the bugs off and give the tank a pat.

Thanks, man.

Don't mention it. It was fun for me, too.

We've gotta do this more often, huh?

Don't have to ask ME twice!

I chuckle and reluctantly drag out the lawn mower, somehow re-vitalized and refreshed.

It's good to be alive!

A "Memorable" Ride

What the hell!!!????
Or something to that effect.
Memorial Day Weekend, 2010.
Yesterday (Saturday) had been a perfect day. I'd snuck
off on Lazzy (Lazarus, my Nighthawk S, so named because
I raised him from the dead) for a short ride, which ended
up morphing into an extended ride. The weather was near
perfect...not too hot for leathers (ATGATT!)*, not too windy,
with a lazy sky the color of robin's eggs. Lazzy was humming
like a swarm of mosquitoes on a sweltering summer's eve,
purring like a contented kitten, running about as perfect as
anyone could hope, for a 25-year-old bike.

Especially for one that had died. I milked it for what is was
worth; believe you me! Not sure how far I ended up going, but
it was damn near close to 100 miles. A superb ride, a great bike.
It was one of those days when you hang on, twist the throttle,
and follow the bike. I was not disappointed. Yesterday.

Yesterday had gone so well, I decided to try my luck again
today. I didn't plan on taking the exact same route, just close
to it. Only this time I was gonna let the Buellosaurus Rex out

of the cage. It started out well, really, it did. Today was a bit warmer than yesterday; even with the visor cracked open a tad and all the vents unzipped on my Vanson jacket. (Remember; ATGATT!) I fueled up; premium, at $3.03 a gallon, as opposed to the regular I pumped into Lazarus yesterday, at $2.84 a gallon. Oh, well...that's the price of performance, I suppose!

Rex was running good—make that GREAT—right out of the gate. Tuning spot-on, it was there, in the groove. I headed North, into Wisconsin, as I always do. Sticking to back and side roads, pretty much the same flight path as yesterday. The sun beamed down on me; beads of sweat were forming on my forehead. I hung a left on highway UE off of highway K and rolled it on.

The stupid things that run through your head—every time I cut left on Highway UE (ooo-wee) I hear Robert Gordon belting out: *"Ooooweee, oooooweee baby, won't ya let me take you on a... sea cruise!"*

I won't admit in public to bellowing the lyrics inside my helmet today or any other day. I'm not under oath here, ya know! I don't think I did it today, anyway. And that is in no way or shape a confession, by any means...

So, I roll on the power as I make my left on to UE (Oooowee!), whack it hard, and the buellosaurus snaps its jaws and stands up with a gutteral snarl...55 before you can say "Boo!" And it's all good, and then...pop!snort...fart...wheeze...

What the hell!!!???

Which is where we began, no?

I could feel power bleeding off. I pulled in the clutch; goosed it a few times; Rs were right there. Let out the clutch; power sagged, popping and snorting again. At the risk of sounding repetitious...*What the hell!!!???*

Now, even a cruise missile takes some time to land after popping through the clouds. I still had quite a bit of speed to bleed off yet, even with the clutch pulled in. Rex gradually coasted to a stop, mere yards from the Highway 142 intersection, where I had planned on turning left again and proceed to promptly whacking the throttle. Ironic, isn't it?

So, here I sit on the side of the road, clutch pulled in, engine idling away like nobody's business, ease out the clutch, and...wugh. Followed by silence.

I pull in the clutch, blip the START button, Rex roars to life. Ease out the clutch...wugh. Silence.

Where were we? Ahh, yes...*What the hell!!!???*

Think fast, MacGuyver; Not ignition. Can't be. Runs good with the clutch in. Safety switch? Ahhhh...Sure. Buells have a sordid history of sidestand safety switch failures. I lean down and pop the two-pin Molex apart; now, what to jump it with?

Now, I must confess at this point, I don't have a tool with me. Not a one. Not even the ever-present Ken Onion Designs Scallion pocket knife I carry 24/7. Nope; it's back home on the dresser top. Why? Can't really say. Only that it is, and I need it and don't have it with me. I search my pockets for some help. No joy. Wait. There's a little wound ring-thingie attaching my Mini-Mag Light to my keychain. I unwind the ring-thingie and untwist it to form a rather awkward U-clip—and promptly poke a hole in my finger that immediately begins bleeding profusely. *Sonofabitch!* My attempts to insert said U-clip in the female side of the Molex prove fruitless. Rats!, as Snoopy would say. Several cars whiz by; not even slowing. A couple of them almost sideswipe me, here on the shoulder of this deserted road. That would truly suck: "Man Found Dead in Ditch," the headlines would trumpet. I gotta get this gear off; it's like 100 degrees in this leather (ATGATT!). I get the gear off. Whew! That's better! Ring-thingie takes up permanent residence among the chirping crickets and frogs in the high grass along the shoulder.

With no Scallion and no tools, I grab the car key from my pocket with the most teeth and start sawing on the safety switch wires. Once I manage to cut through them, I hold the Molex end with two wires in my hand. With no wire strippers to be found, I result to the *Leave It to Beaver* method—my teeth. Knaw, twist, spit. Repeat. Soon I'm left with a chipped-feeling front tooth and two stripped wires. I twist them together, and plug the Molex back in. Suiting up (ATGATT!), I fire Rex up. So far, so good. Cars continue to whiz by as if late for work. Nobody stops; nobody slows. Nobody gives a shit; face it! I ease out the clutch...wugh.

Sigh. Off comes the gear...again.

A Toyota in the opposite lane slows and the tinted window hums down. An Oriental guy, looking quite lost holding a map leans out and asks; "Are you flom Risconsin?"

"Who the hell CARES where I'm from!?" I think to myself, with masked irritation. "No, Illinois." I'm just about to ask if he has any tools, but the window hums up and he drives away, leaving me standing there with my mouth hanging open, mid-sentence. The ability of humans to offer assistance in times of need is staggering.

Think, MacGuyver...Again.

OK...clutch safety switch? I pop the two pin Molex off *that* and curse myself for ditching the ring-thingie. Ain't no finding it in the high chaparral now, baby. Gone is gone. Some little froggie is probably asking his mom right now; "Can I keep it mom? Huh? Puleeeeease..." I pull out the key ring again and find yet another ring-thingie. Soon I have another awkward U-clip and manage not to perforate my finger this time, which is good, as the first perf is still leaking profusely. In trying to jumper the Molex, I succeed instead in popping the whole pin out of the Molex...kewl! I repeat on the other pin, slip the Molex in my pocket with my bloody hand, and overlap the rolls of the two spade connectors to complete a makeshift connection. This time I do *not* suit up. (ATGATT!) Oh, shut the hell up, I mumble. Gear lying in the high chaparral in the ditch by the side of the road, I'm about to throw a leg over, when a bike rumbles by. They stop, unlike the fifteen-or-so cars that didn't even slow down (except for the lost Japanese tourist).

"Need any help?"

I explain the situation.

"You have help on the way? A tow? Need a cell phone?"

Well, no, but I hope this will get it.

A car pulls up behind him and begins to creep forward impatiently, as if to say, *"Move it, bud!"* He's blocking their way. Figures.

"I'm good," I say, and he waves a reluctant OK and rumbles off. "I hope" I add, to myself. "Coulda used your tool kit a few minutes ago," I think, running my tongue over the chip in my tooth.

I throw a leg over, Thumb the starter. Rex roars to life. Ease out the clutch...

Hallelujah! No wugh!

I mumble a silent Thank You to the Big Boss Upstairs as I suit up (ATGATT!) and throw a leg over, ease out the clutch, and roll. By God, it *rolls* this time! Right up to Route 142.

Turning left, I cautiously roll it on—then more, more! Roll it on right up to eighty as Rex bellows out his throaty clarion call, snarling as if nothing had ever been wrong to begin with. (Silly Human!) I whack it hard, like I'd planned on doing in the first place. Stupid safety switches, anyway!

I decide the direct route home is probably the most prudent at this juncture. After all, I'm still a good thirty miles from home base at best. I glance down at the two connectors sandwiched between the tach housing and handlebars, hanging out in the open breeze, and roll it up to a pleasing, throaty eighty-five—stupid safety switches, anyway!

MacGuyver; eat your heart out!

THREADING THE NEEDLE
BACKWARDS

Yesterday was a wash-out weather-wise, with rain on and off most of the day, and heavy cloud cover. We got a deluge shortly after lunch that left standing water in the ditches, and wet roads, the sort of conditions that make you decide *not* riding sounds like a good idea.

I did manage to sneak in a "quickie" right before sundown Friday. The sun had descended to the point where it no longer resembles a policeman's three million candlepower searchlight in your eyes as you grope about blindly for your driver's license, but rather, a calm, tangerine orb hanging as if it were floating, just above the horizon—the kind you can look straight at without going blind. I jumped on Lazarus and took full advantage of the situation, arriving back home as dusk morphed to darkness, bug-splattered and satisfied.

This morning arrived cool, sunny, and windy. The merry little breezes had knocked over a pair of hanging flower stands on the deck, and the trees swayed and rustled. Not ideal riding weather, I thought. Besides, the wife was at work and had left a Honey-Do list as long as your arm (assuming you are not a small child or a Little Person), and woe to he that doth not completeth the list before She of Queenly Stature arrives home—in earth hours, about 2:30 PM CST (14:30 military). I set about my manly tasks and knocked off the majority in short order.

It was then that my MPD* kicked in. (*Motorcycle Psychological Disorder).

For those of you who are normal, I will explain this.

1) You glance at the clock.

2) You judge how much time before She of Queenly Stature arrives home.

3) You divide by how many tasks on "The List" are yet uncompleted and how much estimated time there would be to complete said tasks.

4) Multiply by the minutes this leaves you to ride.

It is, I might mention, irrelevant whether or not you actually complete said tasks—only that you look busy as hell and are hard at work when S.O.Q.S. walks through the door.

By my calculated eye, I had a good hour or more to bust a move. Not wanting to psych myself up unnecessarily, I glanced out the window for a last-minute weather check.

Sunshine.

Billowy Clouds.

Diminished winds.

As I walked out on the deck, I heard Lazzy's siren call: "Dude. I can't breathe in here. It's all stuffy and shit."

Now, cruelty to motorcycles is one thing I can't abide. Why do you think I have *five* of the damn things? Every time I see a poor, abused, mistreated motorcycle, I feel like Sarah McLachlan holding one of those cute, cuddly, one-eyed kittens on TV—"Please...won't you help save these poor motorcycles?" (Close-up of an abused Nighthawk)

I open the door. Lazzy squints in the bright sunshine. I run the mental calculations again. Check; we're good. With time to spare. I thumb the starter; Lazzy rumbles and purrs like one of Sarah's abused little kittens.

Rex sits there, silently. He knows he's being punished for last week's little insurrection. Parts are on order. I know I could probably do just fine, with both safety switches bypassed, but hey; I don't play that way. It's like playing Russian Roulette with *three* rounds in the cylinder. Besides; uprisings must be quelled, examples must be made, sins must be atoned for. Rex is on Time Out. Besides, I'm on a tight schedule here. S.O.Q.S. will be home in a couple hours. No time to waste bickering with Rex. Bad Rex. Bad Buell. Sit.

I close the door, leaving Rex with himself to reflect on his boorish behavior from the previous weekend.

Lazarus has been on his best behavior lately, starting up at the mere hint of the touch of a well-placed thumb, warming up quickly, and purring like a kitten with a saucer of warm milk once he gets there. Today is no exception. I scan the gas gauge; just a smidge over a half-tank. Enough to get me by. But, as any pilot knows, gas in the tank is like money in the bank. I decide to top off on my way out. I snick Lazzy into gear and wend my way out into the street, and out of the neighborhood, stopping at the corner 7-11 for a unleaded Slurpee.

A quick swipe with the debit card and before you can say Boo! fuel is running out the top of the filler neck and down the sides. Not even five bucks—it's like having an extra bandolier of ammo. A minute later I'm on the highway, winding through the gears. This is awesome—cool, breezy, bright blue sky with errant white cotton balls skittering aimlessly across— what a day! I can smell fresh springtime in the air, the fresh crispness of the cool front that has moved in. Lazzy seems to be enjoying it as well, leaning deep into the corners and feeling unusually perky on the throttle. I start out taking my usual route, then arrive at the crossroads of where I usually head north, ultimately going west, then south to east on the return leg. But I'm feeling rowdy today, and, at the last second, cut east. I've decided to ride the route in reverse; threading the needle backwards, you could say. Why? Why not? I've never seen the run from this side of the road!

It's *different,* strange as it may sound! Things seem...well... *turned around,* if you will. I don't mean that in a smart-ass way; things really *do* seem different. At one point, I approach an intersection; common sense tells me I need to make a right turn, but the intersection appears totally unfamiliar from this view. Unsure, I proceed through the light, realize I *should* have turned, but keep going straight to see where I'll end up. This plan gets foiled several miles down the road when the road becomes torn up and grooved by construction and re-paving in progress. Much as I'd like to follow my hunches as to where I think it will lead me, I turn around, not wanting to risk a spill on the rough, grooved pavement. I do a U-turn and head back the way I came, marveling in the beautiful countryside I've discovered and vowing to explore this route further when I have more time, and the construction is finished.

Back to threading our needle...I pick up where I should have turned right before, and turn left (as viewed from the opposite direction. Ah, yes; now it looks familiar. Lazzy is performing spectacularly; itching to cut loose. But we're behind traffic here, and I realize the wisdom in restraint; lean back and enjoy the ride. We blitz on merrily, eventually coming to a four-way stop at the intersection of two country highways. My speed-governing traffic elects to continue straight ahead. Me; I was gonna turn here anyway!

I cut right and roll on the power, looking straight ahead as Lazzy rights himself, I see nothing but black asphalt ribbon, blue sky, and nary a car in sight in either lane. Lazzy ticks through the gears smartly, and I'm in OD before I can even think about it, still screwing on the throttle: sixty, seventy, seventy-five, then I dial in a bit more: *eighty* now. Lazzy's soothing purr begins to take on a howling tone as the twin pipes begin to trumpet out their song of freedom. This is Life; this is Liberty, this is the Pursuit of Happiness...we're talking

HOT pursuit, baby...DAYUMM! Thoughts flash across my mind like lightning dancing in distant thunderheads—Lazzy, under a tarp in some guy's garage for seven years; Lazzy; motor's top end spread out all over my workbench; the bent valves I replaced, the teeny-tiny valve keepers, the lifters I replaced and those that I cleaned and reused. The myriad of valve springs, the cam chain; so small and fragile-looking—all this, whirring between my legs at eight thousand rpm, with the very distinct possibility of grenading itself into a thousand pieces of schrapnel if I've done just *ONE Thing Wrong*...

But, I haven't done One Thing Wrong. The motor continues to howl mercilessly; seamlessly—like a cheetah in full stride, Lazzy blazes on, effortlessly; never missing a beat. Most of my rides on Lazzy up to this point have been shorter, closer-to-home rides. I save the longer treks for Rex. But, something is happening here, today, between Lazarus and I; something unexpected, something unexplainable—bonding, if you will, for lack of a better word. A trust, a confidence. I'm finding myself becoming endeared to this precise little engineering marvel. And something is happening to Lazzy, as well. With every mile, every twist of the wrist, every lean and roll; he runs better. Tighter. Smoother. And then it happens; on that long, winding ribbon of ebony; we become one.

This is something I've only experienced in the past with Rex (and a couple of cars that come to mind). I thought it a special bond between one man and one machine that could not be shared with another—Wrong! Lazzy and I were morphing into a ballet-like choreography; I would *think* "right" and before I could even feed the input into the bars, Lazzy was *leaning* right—a sort of telekinetic Metalspeak between man and machine.

Blips appear on the radar at 12 o'clock, and we end up behind a caravan of four Harley baggers; radios blaring and tiny American flags fluttering in the breeze. We slow and automatically fall into staggered trail position behind them as they belch out their rumbling, laid-back tractor noises;

sort of like slowing down your wild mustang to trot along behind a lumbering herd of buffalo. Still, I find it somehow disrespectful to go screeching around them—like flipping off a brother, almost—so I loiter, hang back, and pace myself.

It's all good. At the next intersection, they bank lazily right, like squadron of B-17s turning on a downwind leg, thundering out radial engine sounds as if they were sporting real Wright Cyclones. Lazzy snorts with delight as I screw it on again and listen to him howl.

Finally, I reach the end of the ebony thread and have to turn off onto a smaller, slower thoroughfare; we pass the very spot, where only the weekend before, Rex tried to put me on foot. I wonder for a brief moment if the ring-thingie still resides in the high chaparral in the ditch; then toss the thought aside as casually as I'd tossed the ring-thingie in the ditch and get back to the business at hand—*riding*. Clouds skitter lazily across the bright sun, shading the brilliant blaze of light for a few minutes, then bid their fond farewells, destined for parts unknown. I wonder for a mere second the hour, then discard the thought as quickly as it came, "WHO CARES?!!" I think. This is what my inner child lives for; to be free, and wild, with the horns of the bull in my hands and the heart of a warrior shrieking out its war cry between my knees! I feel a kinship with the Plains' warrior of the 1800s, tearing across the Great Plains at full gallop, wind in his hair, sun in his face, with a spirited stallion under him. Inside my helmet, I let out a war whoop..."*HOKA HEY!!*"* then, feeling rather foolish, grin and dig in for another fist-full of throttle. If this were a war pony I'd be digging my heels into its flanks and smacking it on the ass with my quirt.

All too soon, south and east begin to look like home. And then, just that quickly, I'm rolling up the drive, gravel crunching noisily under my tires. I open the garage door and switch off the key. I'm greeted with silence, save for the ringing in my ears from the combination of howling exhaust and wind inside my helmet, and the echoed cries of the ghosts

*Lakota Sioux war cry, meaning "It's a good day to fight," or words to that effect; in other words, the battle cry of a fearless warrior.

of a thousand Sioux warriors. Off come the helmet, gloves, and jacket, I roll Lazzy into the stable, but not before I stroke the small of his back, as a Plains' Indian brave might stroke his favorite war pony. Things are different today, somehow.

Rex eyes me warily as I gently walk my steed into the stable. He can feel the magnetism; the bond. And he doesn't like it; not one bit! We stare each other down, "Huh...you're not the only animal in this barn, Hoss," I say and glance at my cell phone. Reality snaps back like a slap in the face..."Jehosephat! That was calling it close! 2:05...She of Queenly Stature will be on her way!"

Moments later, as I'm skimming leaves out of the pool (one of the many anointed tasks on The List) I hear the queen arrive.

"Hi, Hon," she says, "Whatcha doin?"

"Ahh, just skimming leaves," I reply.

"Were you home all day? Everything looks...kind of a mess," she questions.

"Yeah, pretty much. I mean, I went out for a quick ride, is all. I got everything on your list done," I add... (like the child in the classroom who drives home the issue that he did *all* the homework!). "OK," says She of Queenly Stature, and then; "I'll start dinner soon." A sly grin steals up one side of my face as I eye the garage and wink...and whisper, *Hoka Hey!*

THIS LITTLE PIGGY GOES TO MARKET

Well, we didn't actually "go to market." What we did was go for a ride. This time, the other "little piggy" (Lazzy) "stayed home," having been out with me yesterday for a short tryst. It was a beautiful, though windy, day and the Buellosaurus had been ignored long enough, to the point where I believe Lazzy was probably rubbing it in behind my back. So, I pulled Rex out and suited up. I wasn't exactly sure *where* I was going, other than the fact that I was. *Going,* that is.

And so, we do. Rex pops right off, and as I finish suiting up, I let him warm up in the driveway, the big 1203 doing its best imitation of a paint shaker. Gotta love it! Something about that throbbing, guttural rumble that gets me right here. Now, naturally, one does not ride a B. Rex without the earplugs, unless one is a) in a hurry or b) feeling rather stupid. I was neither today, so I pop them in and roll out of the driveway on this glorious day.

Rex seems just the teensiest bit cantankerous out of the gate, likely due to the week long hiatus he'd had. After stopping at the corner 7-11 for a shot of premium, he's back in the game.

Every time I ride this particular beast, I am utterly astounded at the flickability and balance as well as the immediate seat-of-the-pants throttle response; so radically different from Lazzy or the Seca, or even B. Rex when he was still a mild-mannered Clark Kent in horn-rimmed glasses in pre-mod days. Someone other than myself has described the Mikuni HSR-42 carb as feeling like a direct connection between your wrist and the rear wheel; no truer words were ever spoken!

We head out onto the usual route: a sixty-some mile jaunt through back road cornfield country. The fall colors are just beginning to show here and there, and there is the beginning of the smell of autumn in the air. I roll on the power slowly and evenly and settle into a comfortable rate of cruise.

Heading north into southeastern Wisconsin, we pass numerous bikes; mostly Harleys, not nearly as many as the previous weekend. I suspect that the higher than normal winds have kept some at home. I find myself behind slow-moving vehicles. "Relax," I tell myself. "They're probably just out enjoying the weather like you; too bad they're stuck in a cage!" The thought brings a chuckle inside my helmet, and I *do* relax. What a glorious day for a ride!

I find a Harley in my mirrors pacing me through a small town; he catches up with me at a stop light just as it turns green. I've stopped and he rolls right on through, coming abreast of me with rumble as I clutch through second. I put a little mojo in the right wrist; Rex snarls and he backs off. This is a B. Rex here, Mister, not some two-ton bronto-bagger like yours! I effortlessly take the lead and settle into my pace again, Rex thundering out his glorious song in Metalspeak. I crest a gentle rise and brake for a right turn; scanning for gravel reveals nothing to get excited about, so I lean Rex over hard and roll on the power. Rex, whose mind has been wandering some, like a schoolboy staring out the classroom window, immediately springs to attention and before I know it, has blown past eighty—*"Whoa, there, fella"*—and I ease off the throttle a bit and bleed off some speed to a more reasonable seventy as the cornstalks whiz by like the X-wing fighters in a *Star Wars* flick. *Damn,* I love this bike! The thrumming of the big Vee-twin at this speed and rpm is hypnotic and mesmerizing. It penetrates your skull and body clear through to the bone. I could just "set it and forget it" if I had cruise control. The farm smells assail me and I wish this road would go on forever; but I know it doesn't. I brake, bank left, and after a short bit end up at the next highway.

Turning left, I roll through the gears until I wind up behind an SUV traveling aggravatingly slow—50 in a 55, no less! Masking my irritation, I throttle back and keep a safe interval behind the cell-phone-yakking driver as I impatiently wait for the double yellow and oncoming traffic to end. After an eternity, it does—see ya later, sucker! I dip down into fourth and roll it on; Rex leaps forward in a manner that always puts butterflies in my stomach. Now, you have to understand; when I speak of "rolling on the power," this monstrosity only takes a quarter-twist of the wrist to scare the living snot out of you. The entire time I've owned Rex, I've only pinned the barber pole once; once was enough! Rex leaps forward like I've zapped him with a cattle prod, and the cell-phone-yakker-SUV disappears from my mirrors and off the radar like a distant memory. Unencumbered by traffic, Rex settles in to a nice, comfortable eighty miles per hour rate-of-cruise. As we crest a hill, the full force of the winds careening across the cornfields catch me. We are being buffeted about, not unlike an errant plastic shopping bag blowing about the supermarket parking lot. I can feel the wind tugging at my helmet; the strap straining against my chin in a vain effort to deploy itself. Were it not strapped on, I believe it would launch itself like a cannonball right off the top of my head. I tuck my head down a bit and motor on, enjoying this far too much to let a little wind discourage me!

We blaze on, oblivious to the problems of the world, sucking in the sights and smells and sounds around me. The motor is making a glorious drone as we blitz down the highway. Did I mention I was enjoying this? Finally, we come to the next major intersection, where I'll turn left (and southeast). This intersection is always a bittersweet reunion; *sweet* because it's a magical, glorious stretch of two-lane pavement that winds between a heavily forested section containing a nice stand of pine. The pine scent always seems to waft in through my visor and transport me back to the northern woods of Minnesota, where I spent many a summer scrounging up trouble in the woods as a boy. *Sweet,* also, because it is a section of road that always seems to taunt me to push the envelope; my last jaunt down this particular stretch of ribbon somehow found me exceeding three digits on the clock. *Bitter,* because I always know in my heart this is the turn back toward home, and, even though I'm still thirty miles away, the ride is winding down.

As I mentioned, I usually engage this section of blacktop with vigor and a bit of punk-youth exuberance, but not today. As we come to a stop, two bikes are resting at the four-way stop in the right turn lane. Since they have the right-of-way, I pause, to give them the option to go. They take it, hesitantly, as if unsure of their destination. Rex closes the gap impatiently, and I can see one rider is a female and both of them appear to be newbies; evident from the shiny new Harleys to the bright orange safety labels still attached to the back of both helmets like bumper stickers. They eke on up to 55 and totter uncertainly southeasterly at a sedate, geriatric pace in a area where I would normally be tickling the rev limiter on the north side of ninety. I try to calm Rex the way a jockey might calm a thoroughbred: "*Easy, big fella, easy...*"

I think about passing them; all it would take is a quick flick of the bars and a whisper in Rex's ear; but no. For some reason I decide it would probably be bad form to smoke by two obvious newbies, probably scaring the snot out of them in the process, and possibly tainting their view of sportbike riders forever. As the saying goes: *"You only get one chance to make a first impression."* I throttle back and drop into staggered formation behind them and relax; there's still a lot of highway left before home. Rex fidgets impatiently; I know he was anticipating that empty stretch of highway and the surge of adrenaline that parallels a nasty power roll-on, but he'll just have to be patient for now.

Several miles down the road, and the left turn blinkers come on as the newbies totter off down a side road, still giving off an air of uncertainty. Immediately past this intersection is the one I usually take, today is no different, so I slow and bank left.

"Now, Boss?"

"Go get 'em, Rex!"

The Vee-twin between my knees fairly explodes as I whack the throttle, *hard,* the guttural, Jurassic snarl making the little hairs on the back of my neck stand up. Rex lunges forward like a quarter horse taking the bit in its teeth and it's all I can do to hang on—50, 60, 70, 80, 90—*Slow down, boy! Easy!* I can't seem to erase the shit-eating grin off my face, as I ease back down towards a little more legal pace. Rex snorts and shakes his rebellious Buellosaurus head; a true prehistoric meat-eating predator; angry, defiant, and representative of his name.

Tyrannosaurus Rex, loosely translated, means "Terrible Lizard King."

Buellosaurus Rex, loosely translated, means...well, I guess it can mean whatever you want it to. But you get the idea.

Rex seems to relax a bit now; we thunder down the highway with scant traffic in the oncoming lane and nothing but empty, open road stretched out in front of us. Ahh...the freedom and solitude of a solo ride!

We pass a farm near the road and smell the freshly mown hay. Cows gaze sedately through the barbed wire as we thunder by, chewing their cud, staring like bovine village idiots, as the flies buzz around their heads. I can almost hear their thoughts as we rumble by—*"COW-asaki...COW-asaki... COW-asaki"*—if only they knew! All this scenery frozen in a nanosecond mind-snapshot. I roll on a little more throttle as the road inclines, Rex eager to be out of hostile cow territory. We crest the incline and begin a long descent to the major highway we'd gone north on. Rex burbles happily as I engine brake down the slope; downshifting through the gears until we come to a stop. Then it's a quick glance north to check for traffic; all clear, and we turn right heading southbound. Rex snaps through the gears swiftly, effortlessly, and we find ourselves riding formation behind two Harley baggers sporting doo-rags and oh-fishul Motor Company garb.

We come to another major intersection, and I enter the left turn lane; the two Harley riders in the straight lane do their best to completely ignore the noisy brethren sportbike to their left, despite my amiable nod their way. It's as if we were a ghost or apparition. Or, perhaps, had leprosy. The green left-turn arrow illuminates and Rex lunges forward and leans gracefully left. He is obviously perturbed at being snubbed by the snooty baggers and makes his displeasure public with an angry snarl. I find this mildly amusing, but he is a sensitive old buellosaur, despite his appearance. *"Dude, chill!"* I admonish, and he seems to shake it off and forget all about them as he makes a right onto another two-lane country farm highway.

We slow here; caution is the watch-word as winding, shrub-obscured driveways threaten potential danger. We arrive at our connecting intersection and turn left again—closer, closer to home. I ease off throttle, relax, and lean back in the saddle; and take in the sights and smells of an idyllic farm country highway. It's almost too perfect. My uncle, a pastor from Colorado, tells a story of a member of his congregation who had just died; he was asked to give the eulogy. Being new to both the area and congregation, he sought out a little information about the deceased. His widow, between laughter and tears, told the story of how much he loved to ride his old motorcycle. Early one afternoon, after lunch, he told her he was going for a ride; he'd be back in a couple hours. She began to worry as the Rocky Mountain darkness approached with no word, then the phone rang. It was her husband, calling long-distance from a payphone, apologizing for not calling sooner, and for being two states away. "It was so peaceful, so beautiful," he explained, "that I just kept going...I always wanted to see California." (She was laughing now, with tears rolling down her cheeks, as she told her story.) "Well," says she, "you better *damn* well call me when you get there!" She forgave him, she said, because he always told her there were only two loves in his life...and the bike was Number Two.

I can totally relate! There are times when I feel the urge to turn right when home is left, to storm down the road unknown just to see where it goes. Not today; I'd scratched the itch and was content to wend my way homeward bound, although I had been getting more creative as of late about just *how* I arrived there. South is south, and east is east, and you usually wind up "Close Enough for Government Work." We take a couple of detours and end up in the target zone area despite our creativeness. See; it all works out in the end!

All too soon we find ourselves on the last long, winding turn before we arrive back in the neighborhood; I'm hoping there won't be any traffic on the road today. I usually enjoy my "Hail Mary" last-ditch throttle stomp around the long, sweeping curve, tucking in tight while rolling it on. Not today; I join the sedentary queue of traffic and resign myself to enjoying the last few minutes of the ride.

We pull into the driveway and come to a reluctant stop in front of the garage. I swing a leg over the saddle and flip the key off; the thunder stops instantly, leaving only the echoes and background ringing in my ears, despite the earplugs. Off with the gear; I walk around and open the garage door, stow my gear, and then reluctantly push Rex inside, the motor ticking and radiating shimmering waves of heat like a dog in a mill pond shedding fleas. You can *smell* the heat; the fuel vapor smells, the motorcycle smells that mix and mingle, yet I somehow know what they all are; twisted and blended into a mysterious concoction that assails the olfactory senses with an almost overpowering urge to grab a handful of throttle. You know what I mean, right? Sure you do. I can sense it. You're probably sporting a big grin right about now.

Lazarus appears pissed at being left behind today; giving the jealous bitch-eye to Rex, who lounges smugly in his spot, basking in his latest Thunder Road glory. I sternly remind Lazzy he's had *his* day in the sun, plus more. The little Banshee looks forlornly over her shoulder from high atop the extended lift table; *"What about me?"* she asks...*"I haven't been on the road in two years."*

"Patience, Little One...you know your time will come again." She sighs. I doubt she believes me, but *I* know I'm sincere. I got really close this year, actually firing her up before fuel pouring from dried-out, leaking O-rings on the Mikunis made me shut her down for fear of having an unscheduled weenie roast. We both know it's too late in the year to get her back on the road. *"Next year, Little One, I promise, next year..."*

She pouts. She *always* pouts. I hate that. *"Now listen,"* I admonish; *"you were here long before either of these two guys; how many miles did we do then, just you and me? You think I've forgotten? I could've sold you easy when your brothers came home, but I didn't. And I won't. There will always be a spot for you in my garage."*

This seems to satisfy her for the moment; I turn and walk between Lazzy and Rex; I drag a rag across Lazzy's seat the way you might tousle a small boy's hair. He beams up at me, placated for the moment; all is well again.

I stand under the open garage door; the lawn mower beckons with all the appeal of a pair of leg irons. I grimace and roll the ol' ball and chain out into the bright sunlight. As I push the magic button and the garage door lowers, the objects of my affection fade from view like a tramp steamer disappearing on the distant horizon. I pause a moment; visions of Japanese cows and blurry fence posts dance, still, in my mind. A half-grin slides it's way up the side of my face, and on that note I lean over and tug on the pull-rope and the mower roars to life.

MARCH MADNESS

MARCH; I HATE MARCH. March *sucks*. I have many reasons for this astute observation, the first having to do with an old adage; *"March...comes in like a lion and goes out like a lamb."* Only half true. True, in part, because as January with her icy tentacles gives way to February with her wild mood swings, and the huge mounds of blackened snow begin to dwindle in the warm, tantalizing, lengthening rays of sunlight, bringing hope, anticipation, and *March*. In she comes, like the proverbial lion. But she rarely, if ever, leaves like a lamb. Most times she leaves more like a tigress, soft, furry, but far from de-clawed.

March, you see, is *a damned liar.*

She teases us, usually while we are busy toiling at the job or at home, stretched far too thin to break free from the yoke of our labors and go for a ride. Some idiot *(never me, damn it!)* will go riding by, the distant rumble of the motor's thunder will stir and tear at emotions slumbering deep inside you, and then fade away, like the last struggling rays of a sunset being snuffed out by the darkness; leaving a yearning and longing deep within, an itch not scratched.

March has few high points; one being St. Patrick's Day, when I manage to put aside my winter doldrums and enjoy my corned beef and cabbage, boiled red potatoes, soda bread, and of course, Guinness Extra Stout (and perhaps a wee nip o' the Jameson's after dinner—*"always after me Lucky Charms!"*).

St. Pat's also brought the taunting Siren's call of near-60s temperatures, with the heavy dirt-smell of thawing earth, the twittering of a few brave bird-souls, and the warm caresses of errant breezes playing about your ears as you walk about outdoors; teasing and tempting you to just *take off the damn jacket!* and come play. And damned if you don't think about it as you work, but by the time work is finished, the sun is a huge electric-orange basketball hanging low on the horizon, the shadows long and tall, and you realize you need the jacket after all.

March *is,* after all, *a damned liar.*

Two days later came freezing temps, rain, hail and wind— *Bitch!*

March also takes her leave with a bad aura hanging in the air; like the distant, lingering stench of burned rubber or fried electrical wires.

You see, twenty-two years ago, I lost my Dad to March. She caught me napping, off-guard, like a thief in the night. I never got to say good-bye; never got to tell him how much he meant to me. That I loved him. That he was the greatest influence in my life, and the finest example of one that anyone could ever have.

She blew a hole in my heart big enough to toss a cat through, and left me there to die.

But I survived; the wound healed, but never went away. The scar remains, and every so often, usually right after the short-lived enjoyment of St. Pat's, she'll make it a point to remind me, ol' March will. Dig at the scar. Poke at the scab. And I find that it can still hurt. The Jameson's seldom lasts past the end of the month.

Deep in the depths of my garage, the motorcycles slumber silently under their covers, nothing but stale air in their empty, drained float bowls, the gasoline in their tanks going slowly flat. Winter is a long time going here in the heartland. We've already met the first of my pre-riding requirements; a heavy downpour two weeks ago, a true frog-strangler that ended up as a hailstorm. This served to wash away most of the White Death laid down by the city and county trucks, but the roads still remain littered with sand and gravel. Especially in the corners. I start looking and paying close attention this time of year. And the weather doesn't cooperate much either; I find myself still scraping frost off the windows of my truck in the early mornings. Yes, I know some people ride as soon as the snow melts, some as soon as the roads are clear, trundled up like so many Eskimos with their heated grips and other newfangled contraptions. I'm no wuss, but let's face it; to me, riding is not "cheap transportation" nor a *machismo* contest. It's an adrenaline surge, a freedom call, a jailbreak from the Winter State Prison. But most of all, it has to be *enjoyable*. And freezing my ass off, riding on gravel-strewn roads, in high, gusty winds with snow flurries or sudden, ice water deluges just ain't my cup 'o tea. I supposed I *could* ride, just to prove a point, but then Van Gogh lopped off an ear to prove a point, which I don't think showed much in the way of smarts either.

And so, I wait. *WE* wait. Maddeningly slow, we wait, and listen to her damn lies.

As I write this, I am amused by the fact that the plates on my Buell expire at the stroke of midnight tonight...March 31st—only a few scant hours from now. And I haven't even fired it up in The Year of Our Lord 2011 yet.

But tomorrow is April Fool's Day (appropriately enough!), and snow flurries are in the forecast. Likely I will drive over to the DMV over the upcoming weekend and get my stickers, but the forecast doesn't show anything that I might even remotely consider good riding weather for several weeks. While I hate to leave a good plate "un-stickered," I can think of better things to do with half a C-note than stick it to cold steel and cover it up again. I may wait, after all.

In a few short hours, March will be behind me, with the whispered promises of April holding far more credence and truth than March could ever wish to. And we will be here waiting, my motorcycles and I.

April Fool

April broke as the weatherman had predicted—cloudy, overcast, chilly—with one exception.

The snow flurries predicted turned out to be rain. Rain, followed by a warm front moving in.

April 2nd broke partly cloudy; the sun playing hide-and-seek through the clouds. Although the breezes were stiffer than I usually prefer, and the roads still littered with more sand and debris than I feel comfortable with, it was obvious that the joke was on me—I, with expired license plate sticker.

"So," you ask, *"why not take one of the other bikes?"*

Oh...you mean "Li'l Banshee," the Seca? With its bank of carbs lying open on the bench like a field-dressed deer waiting for O-rings? Or "Lazzy the Nighthawk" with his most definitely flat front tire? One of those two?

April Fool!

Ummm...I think they mean me.

April is surely feeling playful these days. Not *bitch-eyed* mean, like March, but playful. Teasing. Minx-ish.

Tag...you're it!

Despite the warming trend on the second of April, I felt

I'd made the right decision. The temps hovered in the forties and fifties throughout the week; the sky would spit every so often, as if in contempt of we two-wheeled brethren, and the winds continued to kick trash and debris around the corners of buildings as if to warn me: "Don't get cocky, son. I'm ready when I'm ready."

This is a game, right? Count me in—I'm playing.

There is a ten in my hand, a seven showing on the table. I'm feeling confident a Blackjack is in reach...

"*Hit me.*"

She does.

The following Saturday breaks, sunny with scattered clouds, highs in the *eighties!*

Busted.

Now, I can tell you without provocation that the punk kid in me was chomping at the bit to swap plates with Lazzy and take the Buell out for a short spin; I mean, who's gonna know... right?

But every day seems to bring a few more gray hairs, and for each one added, a little bit of punk leaves via the back door. It's a calculated risk, yes; but I've already lost one bet this month.

So I stay home and listen to the thunder of jail-breakers who have escaped their particular Alcatraz rumbling in the distance, listening as the sounds of freedom swell and then fade away.

I decide to make the best of the situation. I open the garage door and pull the covers off Rex, Lazzy, and the Banshee and roll them out into the sunlight. All of them are sweating profusely, condensation dripping off the stone-cold steel and aluminum as it sweats in the warm, probing rays of sunlight. I can feel the early spring sunshine beating down on me; I'm warm even in a plain T-shirt. Grabbing a soft towel, I wipe down what parts I can get to without making the towel filthy, then fire up the compressor and have at it with the blow gun at the rest of it. There; that should do it. Flipping Rex's fuel selector to ON, I hear fuel gurgling down to fill the HSRs' float bowls; mindful of sticking floats, I gently tap the side of the bowl with the wooden handle of a screwdriver as it fills. Slowly, the gurgling stops; I glance down at the overflow tube and notice with no small satisfaction that it stays dry. Mission accomplished.

I've had the trickle charger on Rex numerous times throughout the winter, the latest episode just a week ago. I'm confident there's enough moxie in the battery to fire it up. I switch the key on, the headlight, neutral light, and oil pressure light wink on brightly, much the way my dog looks at me when it's time for her evening walk. I pull out the enrichener cable and give the throttle a smart twist and hear the hiss of the accelerator pump as the smell of raw fuel assails my olfactories; deep breath, hold it, then my thumb stabs the starter button.

Rex barks to life immediately, rumbling and vibrating like a paint shaker in my grip. Grinning like a Cheshire cat, I ease in the enrichener and let him idle at a thousand, shaking and twitching like a Parkinson's patient as he tries to do the Curly Shuffle across the concrete.

For those of you not familiar with the older Buells, the Curly Shuffle is the delightful little dance they will do at high idle sometimes moving backwards as much as a foot before you realize the bike is leaving with or without you! Those who are unfortunate enough to experience this on a slick blacktop driveway on a downhill slant have been privy to a very special treat, one which I am lucky enough to have missed. Fortunately, my concrete apron butts up to a gravel driveway, so once the rear tire is in the gravel, I can relax, breathe in the fumes, and listen to the thunder peal. Rex, as usual, does not disappoint. As he warms up, I push the enrichener all the way in and Rex settles into a satisfying lope.

While Rex snorts and growls, I turn my attention to Lazzy. He gets the same wipedown/blow-dry treatment as Rex, flat front tire and all, and soon his carb bowls are gurgling full as well. Crossing my fingers (Lazzy can be a hard-sell in the springtime when he wishes.) I pull on the enrichener and wonder why Keihin felt it not necessary to use accelerator pumps. I thumb the starter and Lazzy wheezes, snorts, stumbles to life...and then quits. I've played this game before; yep, sure enough, the battery quickly runs itself flat without so much as another pop.

I switch off the overly hyper-active Rex and pull the seat, side cover, and airbox snorkel on Lazzy. I'll be damned if a motorcycle is gonna bust my Kharma bubble today. On goes the trickle charger, out comes the air filter, all ready for a snort of starting fluid.

Meanwhile, I turn my attention to Li'l Banshee, the Seca, who is still pouting at not being on the road for three years. With the carb bank still lounging on the work bench, it wasn't likely she was gonna do much besides pout this day, but she deserved a modicum of attention while Lazzy's battery stoked itself, so I wipe her down and give her the blow-dry treatment as well. She seems to enjoy the sunshine and I can't help but admire her classic Eighties look. Fine lines, this one! I pat the sun-warmed seat and turn back to Lazzy.

If any of you as a parent has ever dragged a sleeping kid out of bed in the morning for school, threatening him or her with bodily injury, you'll know where I'm coming from. Lazzy did *not* want to get up today, *"I'm sick!"* He seemed to whine, as I strode back into the bedroom for the fourth time. *"Get Up! NOW. Or I'll give you something to be sick about!"* I threaten. And this time I mean it.

I blast him with a super size snort of the starting fluid, and with battery charger clips still pinching the terminals like a pair of black 'n' red checkerboard lobster claws, I stab the starter button with my thumb—"GET UP! NOW!!!"

He must think I'm comin' up the stairs with a belt or something. *"I'm up!!! I'm up, already!!!"* Lazzy barks to life with a surprised snort, first firing on what sounds like two, then three, finally all four as the idle suddenly climbs and I throttle back. I hold it until the idle smooths and the engine begins to give off waves of heat. I switch it off, and, while it's still warm, I remove the charger, put the battery back in its little closet and snap the side cover back on. Likewise with the filter, snorkel, and seat and then fire it up again. Now fully awake, Lazzy fires right up. Just for kicks, I fire up Rex and listen to the bliss of stereo Metalspeak; boys, it don't get no better than this!

We spend hours in the sunshine; time I should be raking the yard or doing something else productive, but instead spend walking around my metal warriors shining and polishing and preening, every so often letting them roar to life and quite likely pissing off the neighbors. Rex is ready; like a hibernating bear who is now fully awake, he's ready to take his voracious appetite to the open road and eat something smaller; maybe a Gixxer or something similar. Ahhh, but then there's that whole plate-sticker thing—*April fool!*

As the shadows begin to lengthen, I resolve with heavy heart to push them back into the garage, wild horses yet unridden. I whisper to the Li'l Banshee that this year, for certain, we'll be back on the road again, she and I. Trusting, childlike, she believes me. And I dare not let her down this time.

Lazzy seems content to crawl back into bed as I push him back inside. Rex, he heaves a heavy sigh, laden with disappointment, but yet patient. He knows he'll be first out of the stable this year. I thumb the button and the garage door does its herky-jerky dance downward, and I realize even though I lost this hand today, somehow I feel as if I've won.

As I type these lines, it is pouring out; a hard, driving rain comprised primarily of ice water and sleet, driven by high, gusty winds on the back of forty degree temperatures. I suppose, being a glass-half-full kind of guy, I can look at the bright side and rejoice in the fact that it seems to have melted the three inches of wet, heavy snow I woke up to this past Monday morning.

As legend has it, P.T. Barnum once said, *"There's a sucker born every minute,"* and I guess I can bear testimony to that fact by the mere presence of the shiny new yellow reflective sticker affixed to the license plate of the Buell, proudly proclaiming "2011"—yeah, the one I said I should probably hold off on buying. Yeah, that one. Of course, there hasn't been one decent day of riding weather since the minute I peeled it off the registration card and stuck it on there like a postage stamp on a letter to Hell, but we knew that would happen, didn't we?

Seems like somebody had mentioned it, anyway.

I guess buying your license plate sticker is somewhat akin to Groundhog Day; it can be the finest, most mellow February day in recorded history, yet if Punxsutawney Phil sees his shadow, well, you know we're all pretty much screwed. Much the same here, my friend. If Buellosaurus Rex sees his sticker once it's expired at the end of March, we're in for a few weeks more of nasty weather. Go ahead; blame it on me. I brought it on myself.

In any case, the rain continues to beat down on the roof tonight relentlessly, the sump pumps are getting much more of a workout than any of the bikes have had all year. It's a particularly nasty sort of rain, with an accompanying damp, clammy cold that chills you clear through to the bone. Little wonder so many sick and old people give up the ghost this time of year; their spirits probably take a good look around and say, *"Oh, forget this...I'm outta here!"*

I pass the time by tire shopping for the Li'l Banshee. I'm amazed at the way tire prices have escalated in the few years since I bought some for Rex. Seems almost silly to spend several hundred bucks on a pair of shoes for a girl that seldom goes dancing, but a promise is a promise, and I home in on a set for the little Seca that should get her through the next decade, and beyond.

I'm working up a "Christmas List" of sorts for the Seca. She's the oldest of my three "keepers" and has definitely been around the block once or twice, with 44,000 showing on the clock. Consequently, she's showing the most wear. Little Bro did quite a bit when he had her, and I did my share when she was my only ride, but after Rex and Lazzy came home to roost, she sort of got neglected. And it's time to pay the piper.

Last year, it was the new chain and sprockets; installed, but yet unused. This year, it's gonna be new shoes (tires), new carb manifolds, plugs, an oil and filter change, and a carb rebuild all around, plus some larger pilot jets. I figure that will set me back at least three Franklins, probably more; but the old girl is worth it. She is still a stunning little head-turner and a scream to ride when you bury the tach needle up near No-Man's-Land.

Saturday morning broke just the way the Weather Channel predicted; partly cloudy, temps near sixty, and windy, with gusts up in the thirties. I had a mission. She of Queenly Stature (SOQS) had given me my marching orders for this weekend: prep the deck for staining on Saturday, and stain it Easter Sunday after church services, but before Easter dinner. How's that for a tight schedule? I rose early, poured a cup o' joe, and got crackin' with the deck cleaning.

SOQS has a saying: "Men are like monkeys." The first time she used this particular term of endearment, I was, (to put it lightly) deeply offended. I demanded an explanation.

"Well," she says, *"it's like this; men grow hair in places there shouldn't be any. They scratch places that should be left unscratched, and they always want to play instead of work. And we women have to keep the monkeys on task."*

Oh, OK. I'm down with that. That sounds sort of like me. Not such a bad comparison after all, all things considered.

This is why she worries when she goes to work on the weekends (SOQS works every other weekend). She worries that my monkey-self will start off the weekend on task, and then like a monkey, drift off to play. Not that I've ever done that.

Well, you see, it's like this: when it's a nice day out, and SOQS is working, the bikes know it. And they start rattling the bars on the monkey cage.

Not today. I had a job to do. And I was gonna do it. Because, if the deck got prepped and washed today, it would have all afternoon with its high winds, and all evening to dry. Slap on the stain tomorrow afternoon and *voila;* that particular task crossed off the list. And SOQS will be pleased. Not that I'm afraid of the Queen, mind you; far from it! It's just that...well, a friend of mine has a saying: *"Happy, wife, happy life. Unhappy wife, unhappy life."* And like it or not, it's pretty much the truth.

So, here I am, bound and determined to be uncharacteristically un-monkey-like and finish the task at hand. So, I refill the everlasting cup o' joe and haul myself out to the garage for my air compressor.

Now, the reason I need the compressor is a simple one. See, the planks of the deck butt up against each other lengthwise with only a slight crack in between each of the planks. These cracks tend to fill up with dog hair, pine needles, and other unmentionables throughout the four seasons, and, naturally, one would have to be an idiot to stain over it. So the compressor is needed to blow the goop out of the cracks prior to washing down the deck. I wheel the compressor up onto the deck, run an extension cord from downstairs in the laundry room (the only thirty amp outlet in the house), and hook up the air hose and blow gun. I flip the switch, and the compressor barks to life.

"Now wait, Captain," you say (as the compressor tank fills) *"Why didn't you just space the deck planks further apart, and you wouldn't have to go through all this mumbo-jumbo?"*

Ahhh...a very good question! But to fully understand, I will have to tell you The Amazing Deck Story.

The Amazing Deck Story began about fifteen or twenty years ago (to tell ya the truth, I don't really remember exactly when). See, we had this concrete patio out back of the house that butted up to the house and the back stoop. The patio was, like, twelve-by-twenty. And we had a set of sliding glass patio doors that stepped out onto the concrete patio.

Well, see that was part of the problem; the glass patio doors exited a full foot above the surface of the concrete. People (kids, mostly) would step out those doors expecting to step onto solid earth and drop a foot instead. Thankfully, no bones were broken or lawsuits were filed before The Amazing Deck as we know it came to be. SOQS had long wished for a deck, you see, and we had done a bit of price shopping, with ridiculous figures being bandied about like $10,000 or more for a decent sized deck, $5,000 at a minimum. Hell, we couldn't even afford the materials, let alone the labor. So it remained on the wish list, until the day SOQS called me at work with the incredible news that she had found an ad in *The Advertiser* for a give-away deck and should she call them? I told her to hang the phone up NOW and call right away. She calls me right back with the details; this family has a large, three-tier deck they want to get rid of. Free! There's only one caveat; we would have to take it down and haul it away. So what was the caveat, I wondered? Surely people didn't expect to have someone drop off a deck in their front yard.

The next three weekends were spent removing hundreds of deck screws and nails and stacking the piles of wood neatly in the corner of their yard. Numerous blisters and slivers were accumulated, and at least one Makita battery met its maker during the disassembly. But in the end, after three long weekends, the homeowners had the old deck removed for whatever it was they were going to replace it with, and we ended up with a huge pile of treated deck lumber, worn and faded, but serviceable.

Both my sons helped disassemble the deck; if memory serves, they were around six and fourteen at the time. What a couple of little troopers! They stayed out there in the blistering hot sun, helping to remove screws and carry and stack wood the entire time. It was a family project, and everyone did their share, SOQS working right along side of me. In the end, we thanked the homeowners profusely, rented a big-ass U-Haul flatbed trailer, and after four exhausting trips back and forth (Each trip was about 25 miles.) we ended up with a large pile of treated lumber in *our* back yard!

The following weekend began the construction of our deck. The main joists were two-by-tens that I laid out on the concrete. I formed a box section with joists on sixteen-inch centers and laid the planks lengthwise across; and the planks tucked neatly under the aluminum sill of the patio door—a perfect fit! I couldn't have planned it better if I'd tried!

Next came the conundrum about the planks. They weren't long enough to go the full length of the deck I wanted, so I sorted them out by length and started piecing together a jigsaw puzzle of length combinations that would,

a) Fit the required length.

b) Be evenly spaced and matched.

c) Meet the spacing requirements of the joists.

I'm not sure how or why it worked out as well as it did, but in the end, it came out perfectly, covering up the old sagging stoop and cracked, sloping patio with a nice, even twelve-by-thirty deck, complete with two stair sections and railings. And my total monetary investment, other than gasoline, trailer rental, and time was a box of deck nails. I even got the stain for free! My older son, who was working construction at the time, had his foreman give him a couple gallons of stain that was "old and expired." He told him if he didn't want it, he would throw it out. Let me tell ya, it worked just fine; expired or not.

The thing was, in order for this deck to fit perfectly, the joists had to stay on the concrete. And with the joists on the 'crete, the planks stacked up perfectly as well; just as long as I didn't leave large gaps between them. Besides, who wanted to look down and see the ugly, old cracked concrete anyway? So, now you know The Amazing Deck Story and why there are no gaps between the planks.

———

Getting back to The Amazing Deck in the present time, I was busy working on blasting the goop out of the cracks. This was followed up with a thorough sweeping followed by a dousing with the hose and attacking the water with a long-handled scrub brush. I've tried pressure washing before, but it attacks the wood, gouging and splintering it—bad idea. A thorough hosing down with the spray nozzle on the garden hose is a kinder, gentler method and leaves the wood clean and undamaged. Which is where it ended up; clean and undamaged. The sunshine that popped out between alternating clouds combined with the wind began to dry the now-clean wood the minute I broomed off the water pooling on the planks.

Mission Accomplished; I put away the compressor and hose and stood back to survey the carnage. It was not yet 2:00 and SOQS was still at work; could I finally, really sneak away for that elusive ride, the monkey-man inside me queried? The wind picked up even more, at this point, as if to chastise me for even allowing such a thought to enter my mind. I've gotta tell you right here; I do not enjoy riding in stiff breezes on a light, nimble sport bike, especially not gale-force winds like these, which had just upgraded to a Cat 2 in Captain's terms. Better safe than sorry, I cautioned myself, and went about doing a few other assorted things that should please SOQS, who would be arriving home from work soon.

The Queen was indeed pleased when she viewed the squeaky-clean deck, and the fact that the monkey-man had not only put away his tools and implements of destruction, but had stayed on task all afternoon. If I could manage to get the stain on tomorrow; without fail, I'd be in good with the queen. Happy Wife = Happy Life.

An hour or so after SOQS arrived home from work, I happened to glance out the back door, and...could it be?!! The pines in the back yard, while still swaying in the breeze, were no longer rocking dangerously to and fro. The winds had died down, as is wont to happen in the late afternoon/ early evening. Monkey-man seized the moment and having pick-pocketed the keys from the zookeeper's belt, unlocked the cage.

"I'm gonna go for a short ride, Hon. I'd like to at least get out before the end of the month." (This last part a bit sarcastically.)

"But, you don't have your sticker," she admonishes.

Wrong-O, Darlin'...this April Fool played **that** hand last week.

"Yes, I do."

"Oh...OK then... have fun. And be careful!"

The monkey-man inside rubs his hands together and chortles with glee as I pull on my riding boots and fairly sprint for the garage before Mother Nature changes her fickle mind again. The Buell sits on the lift, snoozing, with bikes stacked up behind it.

I quickly re-arrange things and shake Rex to wake him up.

"Huh...whaaa...what?"

"Wake up, you big lummox. We're steppin' out!"

Before you could blink an eye, I had the other bikes back in the garage and was donning my gear. In my haste, I completely forgot about the foam earplugs that are damn near required equipment on the Buell. I thumbed the start button, and Rex roared to life.

At this point, I was pretty happy that I'd gone through my pre-flight two weeks earlier, on that warm spring day that I *couldn't* ride. Monkey-man threw a leg over, snicked it into first, and eased out the clutch.

Lord, it felt good. I did the mental calculations and decided that it had been an incredible *five months* since I'd been in the saddle. No matter; I was instantly right at home. I swung out of the subdivision and ascended through the gears. A mile down the road, I swung into the gas station I frequent, and got the first shock of the new year...premium was $4.48 a gallon! Normally I don't pay attention to the cost of premium; Rex is the only vehicle I own that requires it. It took $10 to top off the tank, but I sucked it up and climbed back on, and headed for the open roads.

I didn't go far, maybe twety-five miles in all. The winds were buffeting me about a bit, and it didn't take long to figure out I'd left the earplugs behind. Plus, Rex was acting a bit peculiar; the first time was when I traversed a bumpy railroad crossing, and my throttle hand twitched. Rex let out a belch through the exhaust that sounded like a gunshot. I wrote it off as a jet of raw fuel from the accelerator pump igniting in typical backfire fashion. Regardless, we kept going. Everything seemed fine, though Rex felt slightly "off;" I couldn't dial in on anything in particular; he was running strong. But when you've been listening to Metalspeak as long as I have, you can sense when something is not quite right. A few miles down the road, I made a left turn and rolled it on a little hard. This time, Rex bucked, jerked, and let out a ka-POW! through the exhaust, and then caught himself and carried on as if nothing had happened. At this point, I was beginning to feel uneasy. Not wanting to end up stranded somewhere, I decided to turn around at the next intersection and head back for the barn. Though Rex behaved himself the rest of the way, I couldn't help feeling something was not quite right.

When I pulled up in front of the garage and dismounted, I let Rex idle for a bit as I doffed the helmet and gloves. He sounded strong, but I still had this "feeling." I can't explain it. I rolled Rex back into the garage into the "on-deck circle" and closed the door.

When I walk inside, the queen asks, "How was your ride, Hon?" *"OK,"* I answer, *"but Rex was acting a bit snarky."* Fortunately, she doesn't ask me what snarky means, which I would have to explain, which also means I don't have to explain *why* Rex was acting snarky, which she wouldn't understand anyway. The queen has a heart of gold, but is a bit lacking in the comprehension department when it comes to things mechanical.

Thinking on it later, I was wondering if perhaps I'd developed an induction leak and was getting a lean backfire, then it dawned on me that a lean backfire would pop back through the air filter, right by my right knee. No; this was an afterfire, through the exhaust can. Two things I know of can cause afterfires: sticking exhaust valves and ignition cutout. There were no other symptoms of an exhaust valve sticking. Ignition cutout, however; that is exactly what happened last summer when my clutch safety switch failed. (*see "A Memorable Ride"*) Ignition cuts out, exhaust header fills up with unburned gases, ignition kicks back in—kaPOW! Could I still be having safety switch issues? I don't know at this point, but it bears further investigation.

———

So, the next day, Easter Sunday, dawned once again, just as the Weather Channel predicted: breezy, partly cloudy, and probably ten degrees cooler. I managed to get the stain on The Amazing Deck, only running out of stain before I had finished the railings, which suited me just fine. You see, several of the railings have twisted and warped with age, so I will be replacing them soon, probably next week, and can pick up another gallon then. The new railings will need to be stained anyway. The lion's share of the work is done. And

I managed to finish up before the Easter ham was through cooking, which translates to perfect timing in my book!

So, April may have trumped me, but in the end, I called her bluff—and won. Though it was a short ride, and not without its troubles, it was a ride nonetheless. And in my book, any ride is a good ride.

The Shoemaker's Children

The Shoemaker's Children...
They go barefoot, or so the saying goes. And so it goes for the bike-builder's children. Case in point; I'm in the middle of two project bikes: my CB550 Four and my VF750F Interceptor. While I'm (conveniently) storing the Interceptor at work, the CB550 is here in the garage being restored, and has apparently claimed squatter's rights on my beloved Handy Lift, putting himself, effectively, up on a pedestal, so to speak. Fortunately, I've managed not to incapacitate said squatter for more than a few days at a time. This is probably good, as you will soon find out.

See, I needed to replace this clutch switch on the buellosaurus. Well, not that I needed the lift for that, 'zactly; in fact, I did that particular dirty deed on the concrete, with inadequate lighting, being flanked by two other motorcycles on either side of me; like being stuck in a small elevator in between two fat men. Unpleasant, but workable.

It was, however, during the rough-and-tumble of installing the switch that I happened to notice (fluorescent trouble light in hand, like Indiana Jones peering into the snake pit) that

Rex was, well...filthy! Disgustingly so. This was my showpiece, my crown jewel! How did I let it become this bug-splattered, road-filmed, dust weevil sitting here? My head pivoted slowly toward the Ivory Tower formerly known as the Handy Lift, and I could feel Rex's Cyclops eyeball, and those of Lazzy and the Li'l Banshee follow suit, like the glaring gaze of a jury returned from deliberations with a hanging on their minds...

I heard Rex utter towards the lift, and the squatter perched on it (low and monotone with the Austrian accent), like Arnold Schwarzenegger in *The Terminator* (to the hapless guy in the vehicle): "Get...out."

I was sensing a little hostility here. Thinking it might be in the best interest for all involved for the little 550 to take a smoke break, I lowered the Ivory Tower and wheeled the 550 off. I knew what was coming next; and it involved firearms and somebody named Sarah Connor. Hey...not in MY garage!

Like the peppy little barber in the corner hair emporium, I quipped; "Who's first?"

I needn't have asked, really. The buellosaurus bullied his way to the front of the line and hopped up in the ...ummm... "barber chair."

"What'll it be, Bub? Shave and a haircut?" I cracked.

Arnold spoke up again: "Your clothes...give them to me... NOW."

This guy was not effing around.

Not wanting to be butt-naked in the garage, I quickly changed the subject.

"Nice night for a...wax?"

Arnold eyed the rag in my hand. "Wash day...nussing clean."

"So what's yer pleasure, Mac? Lube job? Wash, wax, oil change?"

Arnold snapped, "Everysing."

"Right-O. Comin' right up!"

Well, I lied a bit, as I had no filter and only one spare quart of oil. So I turned up the classic rock, raised up the barber chair and went to work; cutting, trimming, and shaving. Well, not really. But something to that effect, if I were a barber. Cleaning, polishing, and waxing is closer to the truth.

This was about 10 PM on a Friday night. Next thing you know, I'm lowering the lift back down to floor-level, and it's 1:30 AM on Saturday morning. Rex swaggers off the lift looking a whole lot more now like Fonzie (*Heeeeeyyyy!*) with a fresh haircut than the Terminator. In fact, his whole attitude has changed.

Fonzie leans up against the jukebox, kicks it at the base, and "Rock Around The Clock" comes belting out; Bill Haley and His Comets singing for their lives...

"One, two, three o'clock, four o'clock Rock
Five, six, seven o'clock, eight o'clock Rock
Nine, ten eleven o'clock, twelve o'clock Rock...we're gonna
ROCK AROUND THE CLOCK TONIGHT..."

Fonzie kicks the pop machine and a dewy, ice-cold bottle of Coca Cola drops out—*gratis.*

"Outta the way, Hot Stuff." I jostle The Fonze out of the way (He shoots me a surprised and offended look...*Heeeeeyyyy!*) and holler, "NEXT!"

Lazarus wastes not a minute. He fairly leaps up into the chair and up we go. I glance at the digits on the clock radio on the shelf and notice, with dismay, that it's after 1:30 AM. "You're gonna have to sit tight, cowboy," I mumble. "It's a quarter to two in the morning. Lights out; see ya tomorrow." His feelings are hurt by this obvious snub: "Hey, man what the...?"

His indignation is cut short by the deafening silence as I push the radio button "OFF," and the classic rock goes the way of the passenger pigeon. A second later, I trip the light switch to "OFF" with a loud snap. The fluorescent lights over the lift ebb slowly to black, giving off that unearthly, radioactive glow usually reserved for spent uranium rods, and as I turn the lock home on the door and prepare to close it, I hear The Fonze noisily slurping away at his dewy Ice Cold Coca Cola.

"G'night kids," and to Fonzie, "Share; you gluttonous pig!"

"HEEEEEYYYY!"

I close the door.

The next night I pick up where I left off, boosting the rear end up in the air with my Lockhart-Phillips swingarm stand (seeing as how Lazzy has no center stand) so I can spin and clean the rear wheel. This seems a good place to start. But before I do, I survey the damages, and I am appalled! If Rex was dirty, this thing is...well, let's just say I feel like a social worker who's just discovered welts, bruises, and cigarette burns on a child. I glance around furtively, expecting DCFS to be pounding on my garage door in the next few moments.

I feel I owe Lazzy an apology. "Dude, I'm sorry I let you get like this," I mumble, to no one in particular.

No one in particular answers.

This is the whole problem with the "rat bike" concept. You're supposed to ride it hard and put it away wet, like a common stable horse. When the bike in question becomes a family member, well...Houston, we have a problem.

Out comes the Flitz, Armor All, Clear View, wax, and an arsenal of other cleaners and polishes. I'm determined to make amends.

I start with the now-elevated rear wheel. ARE YOU KIDDING ME??!!! I must have never cleaned this thing properly from the get-go! I know I did, but I can't believe my eyes. I try to work around the rear drum lever, but it's too cumbersome. Screw it; I'll take it off. Soon, lever, bolt, pointer spring, and adjuster nut are spread out on the lift table. Jumpin' Jehosephat! What a friggin' pig mess!

I dig in with cleaners and waxes. The chromed lever gets the once-over with Flitz, and the barrel pivot and pointer head for the wire wheel on the bench grinder, and then gets the Flitz treatment. I remove a thick layer of grime from the drum housing and apply a quick coat of wax to the black enamel. There. Much better! I reassemble the brake and do a quick seat-of-the-pants adjustment, and move in for the kill on the rear wheel.

Friday night...*a full week later*...and I finally feel like I'm close to being finished. It's been quite a week; I've stuffed rags in places that haven't seen daylight since Soichiro Honda slapped this thing on its ass. I've cleaned and wiped and polished in places an earwig wouldn't crawl. I've cut rags into long strips, loaded them with Flitz, and see-sawed my way up and down and around every coil of the shock springs, and the shock bodies themselves. I've preened and polished bolts that have never been removed, and removed some pieces to polish that never *should* be removed. I even dropped the windscreen fairing down on its pivoting hinge and polished the windshield and instrument cluster! Worse than that; I waxed (*WAXED!*) every exposed square inch of frame. It looks OK for a twenty-five-year-old bike. Even better, for a twenty-five-year-old, $250 bike. Better, still, for a lifeless corpse left to rot in someone's garage-tomb. There's not much I can do with dingy, chipped decals or poor paint other than wax it, but for a rat bike, it looks pretty damn good. If I *do* say so myself.

This bike looks all eighties...like the singer in an eighties Big Hair band. I think about Rex's *Terminator* rant the other night and chuckle to myself. Hell, this bike was probably rolling off the assembly line while they were filming that movie! And Rex wasn't even a twinkle in Erik Buell's eyes back in '85. But time marches forward, and we with it. All we can do is try to preserve these machines as best we can, and keep riding 'em. Riding, wrenching, cleaning, polishing. I'm often asked why I don't have a new bike; like a CBR, or perhaps an R1 or R6.

It's all part of the game, baby.

Back in the day, when these machines were rolling off the line, I lusted after them. Hell, I lusted after *any* motorcycle! I would've taken a Moped as a kid. And when I finally got my first bike at fifteen—a wrecked CL350, I rebuilt it from the frame up. Literally. The frame was bent and had to be replaced, along with both fork tubes and triple tree. Looked damn good, too, when I finished (with a little help from Dad, who shot the Candy Apple paint on the tank and covers!), and was the beginning of a long and torrid love affair with motorcycles. I rode the snot out of that bike on the trails near my house and obsessed between riding and cleaning up after riding...maybe that's where it comes from...and realized that the Beatles were right: "The love you take is equal to the love you make." The attention you lavish on your machine comes back to you, in some strange way. I can't explain, so I won't try. Either you get me, or you don't.

Now, all this is lost on my little brother, who has mummified bugs spread-eagled on his flyscreen that were last airborne when Saddam Hussein was still running about, murdering the Kurds. I wouldn't doubt, that if you looked hard enough, you might find a bit of volcanic ash left over from the Mount St. Helen's eruption. Well, OK, maybe I exaggerate a wee bit, but you get the idea...It was this fact, I believe, that allowed me to score the Li'l Banshee (Seca 550) from him for the modest sum of $550 after he purchased his Buell. It had sat, forlorn and neglected, in the back of his garage for several years; a layer of dirt and cobwebs adorned it, like the trappings on a gearhead's Christmas tree, rust sprinkled about randomly on the headers like sprinkles on a cupcake. Homeless mice had made the airbox their proverbial cardboard box in the alley; the filter their bedding, leaving piles of droppings as tiny little black Thank Yous for services rendered, or perhaps a tip. The polished rim strips of the cast wheel were covered in a haze of dirt and grime, so much that at first I didn't realize they *were* polished aluminum, as they matched the hue of the black hub and spokes.

After trundling the carb bank home under my arm for a thorough cleaning and rebuild, I spent several weekend days at his house getting things reassembled and workable. Lo and behold, after installing a new battery, draining the gaggingly-stale gas, and hanging a new filter in the airbox to match my fresh carbs; she hesitantly torched off and, after hacking up a hairball or two, settled into a smooth, albeit high, idle. After a brief warm-up, I tweaked the Rs down to a manageable level and took her around the block a few times. Enough to give me the confidence needed to run down to the DMV and fork over the hard-earned dough to purchase license, title transfer, and plates for the thing. The very next weekend, I rode her home, all of seventeen miles, but it was exhilarating and thrilling nonetheless; a rebirth of sorts, after a long lay-off. I'd sold my 350 some years earlier and hadn't been in the saddle for a very long time—probably a decade or more.

Once home, I reverted quickly back to old habits, kicked it up on the center stand, and began the daunting task of cleaning almost twenty years of grease, grime, filth, and dirt from this sad refugee. I won't tell you it was easy. Frankly, it was a bitch. The header needed to be sandblasted and painted, the wheels, tires, chain; *everything* needed a thorough clean, lube, and polish. Fluids changed. You name it. It was several weeks before I was ready to hit the road. Little Bro hadn't seen it since the day I'd ridden it home, so when he pulled up in the driveway on his Cyclone and saw it gleaming in the sun, he looked shocked, surprised, and a bit taken aback..."Well; whattya think?" I asked proudly. "I think I sold it to ya too cheap" he mumbled; and I tell you, I've not heard a better compliment to this day.

––––––––––

What's in a name? Names can make or break a person; remember the episode of the Simpsons where Homer changes his name to Max Power, and, all of a sudden, everything starts going his way? I mean, did you ever meet a bouncer or a Navy SEAL named Gaylord? If you did, he probably either changed or altered it, or went by his middle name: "G. Lee Jones," or something on that order. I'll never forget the first day of my seventh-grade homeroom. The teacher is calling attendance, we're all like, "Here," and then she says, "Tutor Ellsworth." You could've heard a pin drop. Again: "Tutor Ellsworth." Followed by silence...and then muffled snickering from the guys and scattered tittering from the girls...but no answer. The guy was clearly not there, or not answering. Which is probably a good thing, because with a handle like that, he was likely to get a wedgie or noogie, or worse, from the class bullies who were, incidentally, now circling like Mako sharks looking for whomever might possess a sissy name like that. For real. You could smell the terror; taste it, even. And, whoever Tutor was, he never did show. This little name-calling charade went on the entire first week; laughter and all. Now, for all I know, he might've been the coolest dude I would ever have met; I don't know, because he never did show up in that class or anywhere else in the school, for that matter. Or, maybe he showed up under an assumed name. Who knows; maybe the sharks got him after all. All I'm trying to say is that his momma didn't do him any favors by hanging that moniker on him.

I oughta know. Growing up with a name like "Kirk" earned me more than one blind sucker-punch by the sharks, or a wet towel on the backside in the showers—just because. Anything out of the ordinary draws attention...and blood...by really mean guys with names like Bill, Chuck, and Jim.

But...*TUTOR?* I mean, c'mon...that's like a junior high death sentence! Just sayin'.

So, what's all this got to do with motorcycles? Nothing, if your ride goes by Nighthawk, or Virago (Meaning a bad tempered, scolding woman. I shit you not! Honest-to-gawd. Look it up!) or Maxim (uhhh...*yeaaaah*) or Ninja. Or one of the Alphabet Soup names; CBR, R1, R6, CBX, CB, RD, RZ, XJ or taking it one step further: Harley Alphabet Soup. Which is a place I won't even bother going right now.

Those are the names the factory hangs on your favorite scoot. Some of them are pretty lame, yeah, and so most of us hang our own pet names on our rides. (Whether we admit it or not.) Now, if you named your favorite bike "Janey," face it: either the bike is really lame, or *you* are. And a bike named Janey ain't likely to win any races, *especially* if it's pink, and is more than likely to be on the receiving end of a two-wheeled cow-tipping than basking in the glory of the winner's circle. (If I've inadvertently offended anyone who has named their bike Janey, my apologies. Therapy is available.) If you *have* hung a less-than-macho name on your scoot, it's not too late. Unlike humans, neither a day in court nor dead presidents are not necessary to change the name of your bike. "Janey" could become *"Max Power"* without so much as a dollar changing hands. And you might find your little pink Rebel suddenly carving corners like an R1. But seriously, dude, change the paint.

"So, Captain, how about you?" you ask, "How did you go about naming *your* bikes?"

Well, I'm glad you asked. See, there are two things you need to know about The Name Game. First, bikes can be either male or female. How do you tell? (Get your mind out of the gutter—it's nothing like that.) There is no set hard-and-fast rule here. I don't believe a V-Max could be female (although I *have* known a few females with the *temperament* of a V-Max, but we won't go there); and I find it hard to envision a Repsol Honda exhibiting female tendencies; but now, show me a couple Ducatis in a street race, and it's not too hard to picture a cat fight, if you get my drift.

This "engendering" process is not black-or-white. Sometimes you have to wait; to ride and observe. And wait, patiently, for these things to reveal themselves. A cat will scratch, eventually. Likewise, a shark will show a fin, if you swim long enough. Unfortunately, many people name their rides without thinking to do what you would do to any human you meet—*just ask!* Many times, I believe, your favorite two-wheeled friend is begging to tell you his or her name. But you ignore all the signs and hang some stupid, fruity name on your pal, much to their chagrin. And embarrassment. I mean, c'mon—"*Janey*"?

Take my Seca, for example. This bike is a female. I can't tell you why, but it is. Now, that doesn't mean it's a "June Cleaver" bike, far from it. More like Milla Jovovich. In fact, the name that ended up getting tacked on this particular kitty cat is The Li'l Banshee...because when you screw the throttle wide open, this thing *howls* like a banshee haunting some forlorn Irish castle, and I, for one, wouldn't want to get in her way. Not I. Recently I watched some game wardens trying to cage a bobcat kitten on Animal Planet. It was treed in somebody's back yard and looked so helpless and cute out there on a limb, until they tried to knock it down with a pole and net it. That cute, fuzzy little ball of fur would likely disembowel you and play volleyball with your freshly-removed liver before you finished calling it a "Nice Kitty."

MeeeYOW!

With other bikes, it's obvious. Take Lazarus, for example (my Nighthawk S). The parallels were too blatant (and humorous) to overlook. Lazarus, of Biblical fame; dead and buried. Wrapped up like a mummy and tucked away in a tomb to rot. Not only dead, but from all accounts, he was smelling pretty ripe by the time Jesus arrived. Lazarus the 'Hawk—dead and buried. Tucked away in a garage-tomb under a canvas tarp for seven years. In motorcycle language, that's *skeleton-time*.

Lazarus being raised from a corpse (a really, *really* dead one, at that) to a living, breathing, live person; Lazzy the bike going from Zero to Hero...well, that's about where the parallels end, but close enough to hang a name on him. He's alive. Quite. In fact, at odds with the rumor of his premature demise hangs the bald truth that a twenty-five year old machine (only showing 9k on the clock when the coroner stamped his death certificate) has just ticked over 13.5K, and is testimony enough to the fact that 1) Yes, it runs. Quite well, Thank You! and 2) Yes, I am riding the snot out of it, despite owning two other daily riders.

Speaking of others, let's discuss Rex. Buellosaurus Rex, to be precise. Now, Rex did not have a name when I purchased him; he was simply the new kid on the block. In fact, at that time, I wasn't sure he even *had* a name. I just referred to it as "The Buell" or "Cyclone." Well, for the first two years, anyway. (See, I *told* you these things don't happen overnight!) That is, until I decided to do the mods to it.

I was actually quite reluctant to rip into a fairly new, leak-free bike that was running like a raped ape. In fact, as I began to turn the first screws, I began to wonder if I hadn't slipped over the edge of the dark abyss and had gone stark, raving mad! But as with other things (pretzels come to mind), once you start it's hard to stop. Soon the item of my hard-earned dollars and affections lay opened in front of me like a ripe watermelon. In went the new Andrews N8 cams, on went the Buell Race Kit ("FOR OFF-ROAD USE ONLY!!!" shrieked the warning on the instructions...yeeeeeah...) including race header and muffler, race ECM, high-flow race air cleaner assembly, and finally, the *piece de resistance:* the Mikuni HSR42 flat slide carb. Uh huh, quite an impressive package. And when I finally buttoned it all back up, it was with some trepidation that I worked up the nerve to thumb the starter button, heart pounding away like it would crack a rib or two...

U u h h h ... r o w r ... r o w r ... r o w r ... **BLABADABBADABBADABBA...**

Thunder and lightning exploded before my eyes.

And there, strolling out of the smoke and mist, swaggered what appeared to be a Tyrannosaurus Rex dressed in electric metallic blue, "Buellosaurus Rex. Glad t' meetcha." He held out one of his tiny, clawed forearms; all the while, popping his jaws and gnashing his teeth. Clearly not one to piss around with. All that was missing was the cigar.

The resemblance to the T. Rex in *Jurassic Park* was uncanny, as he stared about with his beady little red eyes. Not wanting to end up sharing the same fate as the poor goat in that flick, I chose not to argue the issue and let him keep the name.

Once we had been properly introduced, a test ride was in order, at which time he reinforced his personality and smoked the cigar. I was relieved not to pass any goats on this particular test hop.

Like Lazzy and The Li'l Banshee, B. Rex came to live up to his name, and reputation, full force. And now that I've begun restoration on both the 550 Four and Interceptor, I'm paying close attention to signals from the aforementioned as to who *they* might be.

KAY-ZEE KRAZY

We have had many discussions, you and I, of the stupid things I've done in the past and present. Lest you fear I'll run out of material for future discussions; fear not! I continue to reign supreme as the King of Gaffes, as you shall soon see...

It all started out innocently, as most things usually do. The record-setting (and mind-bending) snowfall we received this past winter lay piled in huge drifts on the side of roads, in fields, and basically anywhere else the city plows could think of to dispose of it. And as it began to melt, it grew heavier.

Superbowl Sunday; my Little Bro, Brian, was at home, tuned into the game and minding his own business, when he heard a strange noise. He paused to listen, but hearing nothing more, he carried on, putting it aside until the next morning when he went to leave for work and happened to notice his garage appeared to have no roof. I say *"appeared to"* because the roof was still there—it was just neatly tucked INSIDE the garage!—on top of his Snap-On roll-around, his Handy Lift, his Buell, his Kenny Roberts RZ350, and everything else inside the garage. Including this KZ1000 that was, well, "camping out."

The good news was the car was outside, and the damage to the contents was superficial. The only real victim appeared to be the formerly-mint seat cover of the RZ, which now sported a two-inch gash, the seat foam spewing forth like tissue from a deep flesh wound. The other good news was that his insurance would cover the major portion of tearing down and rebuilding the garage. When my son and I came over to help him evacuate the former garage so it could be razed and hauled away, I dragged a motorcycle trailer along in tow so we could move the bikes and other assorted goodies to a rented storage area. See, like myself, Little Bro works on bikes as a side biz, and the KZ was there because, well...it's a long story. But, I've got time; how about you?

See, this friend of his, Steve, has been itching for a bike for some time now. In fact, Steve himself was poised to buy my very own Seca way back when, and I snatched it out from under his nose. (*No hard feelings, 'k?*)

So, I guess Steve has had his eye on this KZ for some time now, and the owner finally relented, price unknown, but we'll assume for all practical purposes that it was only slightly higher than the cost of dirt. Anyway, Steve scores, and gets the bike over to Little Bro's house for a look-see. After the once-over and a compression check, Steve is now the proud owner of a boat anchor.

You know where this is going...right?

We have a crap-load of stuff to move out of the former-garage. He's rented a rather large van, and I have my pickup with trailer in tow. It's a drizzly, overcast Sunday with temps barely above freezing, and we have some heavy-duty stuff to move. We dig in.

First to go into the van was the Handy Lift. I'd forgotten how brutally heavy these things were; I put mine in my garage eight years ago, it has stayed put ever since. I haven't even moved it to clean under it, despite the small wheels on one end, seemingly put there almost as a mockery. It took all three of us to lift the thing, and when we did, the undercarriage unfolded like a hospital gurney. We muscled one end into the van and picked up the undercarriage and folded it up, darn near losing a few fingers in the process. And I don't say that for dramatic effect; I literally had to yank my hand out of harm's way in order to keep my life-long hobby of guitar playing. Sliding the lift in the van, we next loaded a very heavy twelve-foot work bench Little Bro had constructed out of angle iron. Heavy? Now, why do you ask?

We followed up with his compressor, and other myriad of tools. I loaded the RZ350 in the trailer and cinched it down, filling the empty spaces on either side with other cool stuff. His Coats 220 tire machine went into the bed of the truck. And that was only the *first* trip.

After three such trips, we had the big chunks gone and neatly stacked in the storage unit. It was at this point that Mother Nature decided to toy with us some and unleashed a torrent of ice-cold rain like an Arctic fire-hose as we struggled to roll the bikes inside before they, and we, got wet. We failed miserably on both points.

We looked like a trio of drowned rats, thoroughly drenched and frozen to the core. The only one to stay dry was Little Bro's young son, along for the ride, who wisely chose to remain in the van while the idiot adults tried to drown themselves. We drove back for another load, barely able to see through the fogged-up windows, even with the heat on HIGH and the fan running full-tilt.

Yeah, it was *that* kind of weather.

As we pulled up in front of his house, Mother Nature, apparently unsatisfied with the results of our little skirmish, and not seeing the white flag flying, pulled out the cork. It began to hail—marble-sized balls of ice pelting my truck, lining the streets and lawns like a terrible accident at a ball-bearing factory. We didn't dare exit the truck, and sat there, cold, shivering, and defeated for fifteen minutes as Mom Nature unleashed everything she had.

We were beaten, and we knew it.

When the hail finally stopped, we gingerly made our way across the street, walking on the slippery little marbles the way a child shuffles around his first time ever on roller skates. In the distance, an ambulance siren shrieked as it made its way towards some hapless motorist who had been silly enough to try and drive on marbles; his car-alarm horn honking in that even, pulsing tone that lets all within earshot know that something bad has happened. Little Bro, obviously feeling the sting of defeat, suggested we go get pizza and call it a day.

Amen, brother!

We had already moved the big and heavy stuff. The rest he could get on his own with the van tomorrow...

Except for the KZ1000.

Into the trailer it went; but it wasn't going to the storage locker; no sir. It was comin' with me.

It didn't matter that I had room in my garage for not even a *tricycle;* I had talked my son into shoe-horning it into *his* garage, for the moment.

(Pssst...it was FREE!) As in; *get this thing out of here, make it disappear.* And so, Presto! Into the trailer it went.

So, after a large pizza, and regaining the feeling in our finger-tips, we squish-squished out of the restaurant with our soggy shoes and damp, clammy clothing and took the KZ over to my son's garage for safe-keeping, with the idea that if we *did* obtain the title, it could be a nice resto. If not, part it out!

———————

My wife believes I have issues when it comes to motorcycles. Me, I don't see it that way, but I can't deny that the symptoms are there. See, I can't turn down a perfectly good (Read; FREE!) motorcycle simply because it's missing some pieces and doesn't run. I mean, knock a hole in the case, tweak the frame, and yeah...I can walk away. I'm not *that* far gone! But this KZ was a typical neglected and abandoned project bike that I just couldn't walk away from, even if I *am* working on three other projects!

She sees a scrap of canvas. I see a beautiful landscape painting.

She sees blotches. I see Monet.

See sees squiggles. I see Picasso.

She hears a din. I hear Beethoven.

She sees a rusting hulk. I see a Lawson Replica.

She thinks I'm nuts. I think I'm just...Kay-Zee Krazy!

And only time will tell if she is right, or I am.